THE DAWN
OF MEANING

THE MCGRAW-HILL HORIZONS OF SCIENCE SERIES

The Science of Crystals, Françoise Balibar

Universal Constants in Physics, Gilles Cohen-Tannoudji

The Realm of Molecules, Raymond Daudel

The Power of Mathematics, Moshé Flato

The Gene Civilization, François Gros

Life in the Universe, Jean Heidmann

Our Changing Climate, Robert Kandel

The Language of the Cell, Claude Kordon

The Chemistry of Life, Martin Olomucki

The Future of the Sun, Jean-Claude Pecker

How the Brain Evolved, Alain Prochiantz

Our Expanding Universe, Evry Schatzman

Earthquake Prediction, Haroun Tazieff

BORIS
CYRULNIK
THE DAWN
OF MEANING

McGraw-Hill, Inc.

New York St. Louis San Francisco Auckland Bogotá
Caracas Lisbon London Madrid Mexico
Milan Montreal New Delhi Paris
San Juan São Paulo Singapore
Sydney Tokyo Toronto

English Language Edition

Translated by Isabel A. Leonard
in collaboration with
The Language Service, Inc.
Poughkeepsie, New York

Typography by AB Typesetting
Poughkeepsie, New York

Library of Congress Cataloging-in-Publication Data
Cyrulnik, Boris.
   [*La Naissance du sens*. English]
   The Dawn of Meaning / Boris Cyrulnik.
      p. cm. — (The McGraw-Hill HORIZONS OF SCIENCE series)
   Includes bibliographical references.
   ISBN 0-07-015044-3
   1. Language acquisition. 2. Meaning (Psychology).
   3. Animal communication. 4. Human behavior.
   5. Evolution (Biology) I. Title. II. Series.
P118.C9513 1993   92-29665
401'.93—dc20

The original French language edition of this book
was published as *La Naissance du sens*, copyright © 1991,
Hachette, Paris, France.
Questions de science series
Series editor, Dominique Lecourt

 This book is printed on recycled, acid-free paper containing a minimum of 50% recycled de-
inked fiber.

TABLE OF CONTENTS

Introduction by Dominique Lecourt   7

I. From animal to human   23
   A dog's world.   23
   The sensitive period.   28
   Beauty and the beasts   37

II. Finger pointing   47
   The first word.   47
   Autistic children and "closet" children.   53
   The ontogenesis of the mug   60

III. Objects of attachment   67
   The teddy bear function.   67
   The smell of the other   74
   The first smile   81

IV. Freedom through speech   87
   Nature nurtured.   87
   Taboo: successful incests.   97
   The human adventure of speech 104

Bibliography 113

INTRODUCTION

For a long time, people have found ways to over-humanize animals in order to rid themselves of their worst fears and find a common bond in mutual veneration. Paleontology has taught us that prehistoric peoples, beginning in the Upper Paleolithic era, tried to work out "a certain image of the universal order" (André Leroi-Gourhan) by creating cave paintings of symbolic figures drawn essentially from the animal world: bison, horses, the great cats, rhinoceroses, and so on. Differences in interpretation, which for decades have caused ethnologists to argue over the significance to be accorded to "totemism," have revealed the animal kingdom as a bottomless reservoir of labels that "uncultured thinkers" could use for their social categorizations. Animals, both familiar and fabulous beasts, are found everywhere in the great mythologies, from the Cretan minotaur to the plumed serpent of the Aztecs; the bodies we see are fashioned by mortals to the point of being misshapen beyond recognition by our visceral fears and relentless yearnings.

The Greeks, with the notable exception of Epicurus (341–270 B.C.), took a philosophical approach and treated this cult with pure contempt or simple condescension. When Plato (428–348 B.C.) spoke of animals in *Timaeus*, he made them sound like degenerate human beings: "But the race of birds was created out of innocent light-minded people, who, although their minds were directed toward heaven, imagined, in their simplicity, that the clearest demonstration of the things above was to be obtained by sight; these were remodelled and transformed into birds, and they grew feathers instead of hair." It is no surprise that the concern for zoological classification remained foreign to a thinker who was so carried away by metaphor.

Aristotle (384–322 B.C.), his disciple, distanced himself from this view and is justly regarded as the founder of "natural history." His observations on animals, from bees to sharks, cover over five hundred different species including a hundred and twenty species of fish and sixty species of insects; they testify to his meticulous concern for accuracy. But we should not lose sight of the intent behind this immense inquiry: it was not description for description's sake. Rather, Aristotle wanted to prove that there was an "intent," a "design," in the structure of living organisms. This intent points not to the act of a Creator, but to the existence of a single and unique scale of being which, by increasing degrees of perfection, "rises" from inanimate objects to plants, then to animals and humans. The latter are animals but "reasonable animals." If the "nurturing soul" exists in plants as in animals, and if, moreover, all animals have a "sensory soul" through which they receive sensations and feel pleasure and pain, only humans are assumed also to have an intellect.

Western philosophy took centuries to free itself from the "anthropocentrism" implied by this conception—particularly as it was reinforced in Christian theology by the passage in Genesis which says that God created us in His image and after His likeness to "have dominion over the fish of the sea, and over the fowl of the air, and over the cattle, and over all the earth, and over every creeping thing that creepeth upon the Earth." The succession of creative acts establishes a discontinuity between humans and animals. If human beings, through their immaterial and immortal "intellective souls" (St. Thomas) are the only beings to share in divine nature, animals suffer a kind of radical ontological discredit. Yet humans are and will always remain animals, and for a very long time we were haunted by the inner threat of our bestial natures. Michel Foucault (1926–1984) clearly showed the nagging presence of this phantasm in the heart of the classical age, at the time when Western "reason" was being defined. "Madness," he wrote, citing Jean-Étienne Esquirol (1772–1840), "borrows its face from the mask of the beast." This obsession was rooted "in the ancient fears that, since antiquity—and particularly since the Middle Ages—have given the animal world its familiar strangeness, its menacing marvels, and the whole weight of its burdensome anxiety." And yet, from that point on, the animal in humans no longer reflected some mysterious beyond; it is our madness in the natural state. Lautréamont (1846–1870), after Immanuel Kant (1724–1804), would give further expression to the force of this Western conviction of Christian origin: the animal belongs to human "counter-nature," to a negativity which, by its bestiality, jeopardizes what is supposed to be the order and wisdom of Nature, beginning with that of humans.

In any event, to the ancients this line of thinking went hand in glove with the geocentrism on which, in the 2nd century A.D., Ptolemy (Claudius Ptolemeus) conferred its mathematical patent of nobility. When taken up by the theologians, it meant that, by the will of the Creator, the finality or teleology of nature placed human beings at the summit of creation, just as the same will had set a motionless Earth in the center of the celestial orbs which constituted the cosmos. It is all the more remarkable that the toppling and subsequent fall of geocentrism in the early 17th century did not lead philosophers to dislodge humans from the preeminent position they had reserved for themselves in what would very shortly be called the "natural economy." Quite the contrary: as it turned out, animals were to suffer from the structure of modern physics. As soon as it appeared necessary to identify matter with extension in order to divest movement of any internal mysterious finality and apply mathematics to it using the brand new "analytical geometry" approach, the distinction between thinking substance and extended substance had to be clear and distinct; within the redrawn conceptual framework of creation, the logical result of such a distinction was to deny animals all ability to think. And so it was, quite consistently, that René Descartes (1596–1650) treated animals like machines.

In his famous letter to Newcastle dated November 23, 1646, the philosopher confronted the difficulty head-on. After explaining that "words or other deliberate signs" are the only "external actions" which testify to the existence in our bodies of a "thinking soul," he showed that this criterion excludes the "speech" of parrots but also the "signs" of the magpie saying hello to its owner: "It would be the impulse of hoping to be fed if it had always been accustomed to receiving some delicacy when the word was spoken." The same applies to everything that "dogs, horses, and monkeys" are made to do. In fact, René Descartes concluded, "No animal has ever been found that is so perfect as to use certain signs to communicate to other animals something that was not in some way related to its passions." To those who objected that "animals do many things better than we," he replied: "Indeed, this proves that they act naturally and as if moved by springs, like a clock that tells the time more accurately than our own judgment can." And so, swallows and honey bees, monkeys, dogs, and cats all act like living clocks.

It was with Michel de Montaigne (1533–1592) that René Descartes expressly took issue, and with numerous passages in his *Essays*, particularly in the "Apology for Raimond Sebond," that denounce anthropocentric arrogance. "Presumption," wrote the moralist de Montaigne, "is our natural and original malady. The most calamitous and frailest of all creatures are human beings, and ever the most prideful." Why should we consider that animals simply do not think? What entitles us to say that the lack of communication between them and us is their fault? We "do not understand the Basques or the cave dwellers," yet do not draw such conclusions; for all that, we do not assume that they are unable to communicate with each other, which is the assumption we make about animals. De Montaigne quotes the great poem of Lucretius (98–55 B.C.): "Wordless flocks and wild beasts by different cries express the fear, the pain, or the pleasure they feel."

There follows a spate of examples designed to prove the existence in animals of various languages differing according to the species, and feelings similar to ours that are expressed by appropriate expressions and gestures. "We must conclude that similar effects derive from similar faculties, and hence admit that this very same speech, this same voice that we use to act, is also that of the animals."

Like Epicurus and Lucretius, de Montaigne helps us see why anthropocentrism persisted throughout the 18th century. It cannot be ascribed solely to the thinking of the naturalists, which remained hierarchical, from Carolus Linnaeus (1707–1778) and Georges Buffon (1707–1788) to Étienne Geoffroy Saint-Hilaire (1772–1844) and Jean-Baptiste Lamarck (1744–1829). It reflects a "presumption" that is not unrelated to the image human beings are anxious to form of their own thinking and to the illusion they cultivate of the sway they claim to hold over such thinking and over the whole world.

It was not until the turn of the last century that the work of Charles Darwin (1809–1882) dealt a decisive blow, in theory, to this anthropocentrism. Sigmund Freud (1856–1939) would refer tersely to it fifty years later as a "narcissistic wound." With an ironic turn of phrase, Charles Darwin showed that he was aware of the step he had taken: "If man had not been his own classifier, he would never have thought of founding a separate order to place himself in it," he wrote in 1871 in *The Descent of Man*. Human-kind ceases to appear as the early promise of animality, albeit inaccessible; conversely, animality ceases to be considered as something that forever embodies the risk of human downfall, the insidious threat of human degeneration.

The next year saw the publication of *The Expression of the Emotions in Man and Animals*, which continued the insights contained in the previous work as well as in the chapter on "Instinct" in the *Origin of Species* (1859). The work is based on a philosophy of continuity: Charles Darwin denies any qualitative or essential difference between humankind and animals, even though the former appears to have far fewer instincts than the latter.

Darwin was to take one further step that would prove to be fraught with consequences. He stated that the entire range of cognitive capacities of humans was already present in animals: memory, but also abstraction, the ability to conceive general ideas, a sense of beauty, and self-awareness—at least in an embryonic state. While of course he notes that they lack language, this does not appear to him to manifest a true discontinuity. He concludes: "Great as the difference may be between the spirit of man and that of the highest animals, it is only a difference of degree and not of quality."

Georges Canguilhem very correctly noted not long ago that the Darwinian "psychology" of animals differed very little from that attributed to them by Michel de Montaigne and the ancients with greater or lesser degrees of imagination. Conclusion: "Anthropocentrism is easier to reject than anthropomorphism." More precisely, in rejecting anthropocentrism Charles Darwin had to pay the price of renewed anthropomorphism.

The fascination of Boris Cyrulnik's research lies in the fact that it takes up this very issue and gives thinkers the wherewithal to resist sliding down the slippery slope of anthropomorphism; in this field he completes the Darwinian revolution. Not surprisingly, he makes fruitful connections with a few other directly or indirectly related extensions (animal ethology, child psychology, and even embryology and the neurological sciences). He introduces a new slice of knowledge by entering the hitherto unexplored field of "human ethology." In a shock wave, he begins to shake up settled ideas and upset certainties in a number of allied disciplines such as psychology, anthropology, and even sociology.

The story, which begins with Charles Darwin, marked by the contradiction we mentioned above, opens up several avenues of research. The most important is the constitution of ethology which will henceforth have to be termed "animal ethology," whose origins are usually traced back to an article published in 1910 by the German zoologist Oskar Heinroth. Studying the behavior of animals, particularly ducks, in their natural environment, he noted the existence of "motor behaviors" that are just as specific to a given group as any physical characteristic. Moreover, it seemed to him that these behaviors changed less rapidly in the course of evolution than most morphological features. Konrad Lorenz (1903–1989) would later refer to this article to designate this "fixed form" as an "innate behavioral pattern." Thus he opened the way to the immense body of observations that has accumulated over the last half century: not only Lorenz, who was awarded the Nobel Prize in 1973, but Irenäus Eibl-Eibesfelt, Nikolaas Tinbergen, and Desmond Morris brought this fascinating discipline to the attention of the general public.

But, as Boris Cyrulnik notes, the term "innate," which rapidly became a noun, (and its opposite, "acquired") sent many "thinkers" down a metaphysical blind alley as soon as they sought to use the results obtained by certain investigators to extrapolate from animals to humans in a sort of reverse anthropomorphism, which was overly respectful of Darwinian "continuity." Charles Darwin flew in the face of prevailing doctrine by humanizing animals, while these "thinkers" applied themselves to animalizing humans. This flawed reasoning was all the more serious in that, at the very same time, the science of molecular genetics was being developed which could have lent credit to the idea that specific "genes," identifiable one by one, might be assigned to the control of this or that human behavior. So it was that, in the late 1960s, animal ethology was enrolled in the service of "sociobiology" invented by the great Harvard zoologist Edward O. Wilson and by Richard Dawkins. Human behavior appeared to be ruled by a genetic machinery whose determinism was as strict as that presumed to govern the lives of bees and baboons. Anthropomorphism therefore became genetic or, if you will, molecular, and people started to speak of "altruistic" or "selfish" genes. If we consider the direction that natural selection is taking, wrote Dawkins, "it seems to follow that everything which has evolved must be selfish." So the individualistic values of American society were enshrined by science and haloed with the mystery of a hidden inwardness! Stephen Jay Gould showed the overt or latent racism toward which some of these theoreticians were leaning, and even unwittingly defending, when they advanced without a scrap of evidence and at the price of manifest simplifications the idea that there could be a gene for intelligence or even a gene for homosexuality, criminality, or schizophrenia. It is easy to understand how a discipline that would end up by "taking morality away from the philosophers and biologizing it" would be a runaway success. We can also see why there would be a puritan moralistic backlash driven by Protestant fundamentalism that would quite successfully attack "Darwinism," caricatured in this way, in the early 1980s.

The much flaunted materialism of sociobiology was in one sense a logical successor to Darwinian thinking, but Edward Wilson, whatever the great value of his research, eventually interpreted it in an extremely reductionist way, saying nothing about our true ignorance of the role of genes in the determination of behavior in both animals and humans. He used ethologic research to gloss over the complex realities of the development of every life form; the weight of epigenesis was held to be negligible as a matter of principle.

By contrast, human ethology, combined with the results of contemporary studies on the development of the nervous system as discussed by Alain Prochiantz in *How the Brain Evolved* (1992), focuses on these realities. With regard to animal observation, it returns to the "objectivist" precepts of the founder of animal psychology, Conwy Lloyd Morgan (1852–1936), and the original inspiration of Konrad Lorenz and Nikolaas Tinbergen. However, this research is taking a second path which is also an outgrowth of Darwinism.

This path was opened by Darwin himself with the publication in 1877 of *A Biographical Sketch of an Infant*, a work compiled from material gathered since 1837 on the natural history of infants, of which the first subject was his firstborn, William. In it Darwin traces the evolution of several emotions such as anger, fear, pleasure, and affection; but he is particularly interested in the appearance and development of language and the preverbal signals of the baby.

In actual fact, he was publicly preceded in 1871 by one of the most prominent disciples of Herbert Spencer (1820–1903), the American John Fiske (1842–1901) in *The Meaning of Infancy*. Here, Fiske made a comparative study of infancy in phylogenesis and classified animals according to whether they were mature at birth (those born "quite grown up" as Jean-Jacques Rousseau (1712–1778) charmingly put it in his *Discours sur l'origine de l'inégalité parmi les hommes* [Discourse on the Origin of Inequality]) or whether they have to go through a maturing period before they are able to perform all their functions. Only the "higher" animals have an infancy, explained John Fiske, and this is affirmed as being a result of evolution. This incompleteness is particularly marked in *Homo sapiens*, the species whose infancy appears to be the longest of all beings compared to the total duration of its development. This has a decisive effect on the organization of human behavior: humans "require supervision and aid for some time." Moreover, John Fiske saw this incompleteness as being a factor in evolution: his theory is that the necessary existence of a family to protect the child accounts, by this prolonged epigenesis, for the transformation of the human brain and the psychological gap between the chimpanzee and the human, although zoologically it is a minimal one.

Though the relationship between the size of the brain and intelligence is still enigmatic and plagued with wild notions, the pioneering work of Henri Wallon (1879–1962) and that of Jean Piaget (1896–1980) and his school of child development have given experimental support to understanding it. But to do so they had to distance themselves from other followers of Charles Darwin such as the psychologist James Baldwin (1861–1934) who, in his famous *Mental Development in the Child and the Race*, based on the work of the great German naturalist and militant evolutionist Ernst Haeckel (1834–1919), chose to see the development of the child as a "recapitulation of the recognized phases in the development of animal series." According to Baldwin, the human child races through all the adult forms through which our ancestors passed. This finalized "evolutionism" once more established a rigidly predetermined direction in the ontogenesis of human beings. And in its wake, we saw the resurgence of animality in the core of madness, although in a new sense: as the very essence of the "disease" of a deranged person now considered the victim of "arrest" or "regression" in the process of "normal" development. Even Sigmund Freud was on occasion beguiled by the charms of this pseudo-Darwinian scheme.

Rejecting anthropomorphism and anthropocentrism alike, and setting itself at the crossroads of the research paths created by this dual rejection, the thinking of human ethology promoted by Boris Cyrulnik deliberately subjects itself to an internal tension that has proven to be extremely fertile. Indeed, by the emphasis it places on epigenesis specific to humans, it has been constrained to deal with the issue of "meaning," the bane of linguists. But far from following the path of any formal type of semantics, where it would be exposed in vain to having to achieve the impossible with regard to meaning (like trying to "square the circle"), it sticks to its "developmentalist" standpoint; hence its comparatist interest for etholinguistics. For the same reasons, it must pay attention to the "accidents" that affect the dawn of meaning in humans. Many are the tragedies that bar our children from the "adventure of speech"! This thinking thus draws on the lessons of psychiatry which, since it operates at the interface of meaning and body, cannot fail to encounter some degree of psychoanalysis. This thinking tolls the knell of behaviorism which, with sociobiology, had obtained a new lease on life and which remains so powerful in institutions where psychologists have to have their professional say. Decidedly, human behavior will never be explained by a scheme that reduces it to a "stimulus-response game"! Even animals, as we shall see, already muddle this trivial interplay considerably from the time of their simplest perceptual activities.

I will now leave the reader to the pleasure of reading a text whose playfulness—the author puns with the sheer pleasure of enjoying his new freedom —appears in the writing as the discrete mark of its philosophical character. The reader will hear the echo, amplified by concrete observations that are sometimes stupefying, often poignant, and always disconcerting, of one of these Baroque aphorisms whose secret was known to Ludwig Wittgenstein (1889–1951): "If a lion could speak, we would not be able to understand it."

Dominique LECOURT

I
FROM ANIMAL
TO HUMAN

A DOG'S WORLD

My dog and I are the owners of a Louis XIII armoire.
It resides in the dining room and is massive, heavy,
dark, austere, and majestic. I fully understand why he
takes pains to avoid it and make his way around it. It
has a dissuasive geometry—you don't want to bump
into it! Yet this is pure illusion because my dog has
never seen this Louis XIII armoire; he will never see
a Louis XIII armoire or a Louis Philippe armchair or
a Directoire desk. What does Louis XIII mean to a
dog? And this armoire, "my" armoire, the one that
comes from my wife's family, that her aunt gave her
one day, pointing out, with the air of one who knows
of what she speaks, that it was a "period piece," an
heirloom that, I remember well, had to be transported
with the greatest of care. No, my dog never met that
armoire because it is soaked in words, marked with

feelings, a silent witness to a whole history that will always be alien to him.

This "thing," because it occupies a place in "my" world, appears to me as an "object" of this world: a reality that is not only located in the physical space and time that I *do* share with my dog, but anchored in many a sensory network and flooded with waves of meaning that give it consistency in our eyes, that of "our" dear old Louis XIII armoire. Can we then say that my dog confines himself to perceiving the "thing" as such, the "thing-in-itself," that he would stumble on its raw existence or bump into its "pure" physical being: its imposing shape, its volume, its density, its neutral properties? This is anthropocentrism turning into anthroposnobbism! Just because his "world" has none of the meanings that give shape, substance, and flavor to my world and that of my wife and her aunt and any friends who drop in, why should his world be a sensory desert? But then, how could we prove the contrary? Am I able to wipe out any trace of humanity in myself and turn into a dog or, in an act of communion, a "dog spirit"? It is probably impossible for me to acquire a canine view of the world through my imagination, but at the very least I can manipulate certain things in a few simple ways that will prove that this dog's world is not reducible to the physical universe, any more than my world is. He too sees his world as being filled with "objects," but they are "doggy objects." For example, I need only place a chunk of meat in my Louis XIII armoire, and instead of walking around it my dog will attack it and yelp at it; he will drool, growl, and bark; the piece of furniture will have lost its apparent neutrality and turned into a meaningful obstacle for him, although this meaning is still very close to biological stimulation.

This is what the animals' "world" looks like— imbued with meaning, even if the meaning is not ours. Observations by ethologists give the lie to the concepts of those philosophers and psychologists who see animals as mere machines driven by the iron law of "stimulus-response." As soon as it perceives, the animal gives meaning to the things of which its world is made. It takes material from the physical universe, from which it constructs its own "objects."

Let us take the example of the sensory activity that seems to have the worst reputation and is supposed to be the crudest: the sense of smell. Mammals are champion smellers, except for humans, who are very weak in this respect. Perhaps our reason for despising this sense is that we want to widen the gap, so indistinct yet so real, that separates us from our close cousins, the nonhuman primates.

Take the male butterfly: the presence of a sexually receptive female will communicate itself to him over a distance of seven miles, and he will fly to the side of his lady love! Today we understand very well how this apparently miraculous feat is accomplished: the female gives off pheromones, those olfactory molecules secreted by exocrine glands. The receptor for these hormones, instead of being located in the same individual, as is the case for growth hormones for example, is in another organism, in this case the male butterfly, who perceives the presence of the molecule with his antennae. He then makes a swaying movement in space; two or three movements are enough for him to gather and pinpoint the information. Then he takes a bearing and lands directly by the right female! One can observe the same process in a feeding shark. If you place a drop of blood in the sea, the blood will dilute. The shark has an ultra-sensitive radar system by which it can detect the presence of blood in extraordinarily minute concentrations: one molecule per cubic meter of water! It too makes its way very quickly to the source of the information. (The reader is strongly advised not to confuse a shark with a butterfly, however.)

Turning now to the sense of hearing, let us take a look at birds. They are capable of astonishing prowess when it comes to sound. When their calls are tape-recorded and analyzed, "sonograms" can be printed to plot the high and low frequencies, providing a graph of actual call structures with distinctly segmented sequences; in this way you can see an amazing degree of synchronization between birds that are calling back and forth to each other. The most remarkable feature is that part of the call is characteristic of each species, representing its sound signature. And individuals of the species in question recognize this call without the slightest hesitation. Although each individual can surround this structure with a few "personal" variations, these discrepancies never alter the part of the call which is genetically programmed in. The observations I made on repeated occasions with my students on gulls on the island of Porquerolles (off Toulon) have taught us a great deal: gulls perceive actual sound structures which trigger different behaviors: hailing calls, triumphal calls, squawks of alarm, mating calls, and so forth. A gull's perception does not fit the idea of mere reception of information: it appears to be finely structured and actively structuring. It manifests the existence of an actual sign language in which gestural spatial signals are articulated with the acoustic and visual signals. When British gulls land in Hendaye, none of their French fellow gulls from Porquerolles will have anything to do with them. The idea of a kind of perception which is merely "receptive" and passive will not account for such phenomena.

But let us move on to the "noblest" of senses: the sense of sight. Here, birds are indisputably the champions, but it is not only at their prodigious visual acuity that we must marvel. A classical observation by 1973 Nobel Prize winner Nikolaas Tinbergen on gull "decoys," allowed their perception to be analyzed in much finer detail. The famous ethologist found that the baby gull, as soon as it has rubbed the inner surface of the egg to break the shell and stagger out, will unfailingly make its way to an adult gull and tap the red spot on its beak located at the root of its lower mandible. A strange and mysterious ritual! Tinbergen went to work to build a cardboard gull that reproduced the complete image of the bird. And he found that the young bird would just as surely tap the decoy on the red spot he had painted. A textbook case which seems to argue in favor of the "innateness" of this behavior, since no learning could have preceded this spontaneous movement.

THE SENSITIVE PERIOD

Questions have been asked about Nikolaas Tinbergen's method. Why take the trouble to reproduce the image of the bird as faithfully as possible with scissors, cardboard, brushes, and paint? Would that not be presupposing that the bird's perception was identical to the perception we have in our human world? Could it not be that a gull seen by a gull is very different from a gull seen by a human? Going on this hypothesis, we constructed another experiment, technically a simpler one, which led to very different conclusions. Instead of scrupulously reproducing the human image of the gull, we simply took a few wooden sticks and pieces of cardboard on which we painted round spots of different colors. In this way we were able to pinpoint what was actually stimulating the baby gull: a particular arrangement of colors. The next step was to make comparisons. When gray was combined with black, only a small number tapped the spot with their beaks; there was an improvement with blue and green; and they did much better with red and black. There was ninety percent success with yellow and red, the "real" colors on the adult gull.

This proves that the "stimulus" is not a simple one; the baby gull's response is not "built in" and predetermined like a reflex, as its response may vary and, even in the most perfect case, ten percent of birds may not be stimulated at all. What stimulates them is a colored shape, which suggests, biologically speaking, an "interpretation" manifesting some degree of freedom relative to the immediacy of the stimulus coming from the outside world; "interpretation" means variations and . . . errors.

When we observe an animal that is supposed to be relatively "intelligent," we see that this "escape" from the constraints of the environment is amplified. An ingenious experiment was done on macaques in a large monkey house laid out to simulate the natural environment. A number of movie screens were set up onto which faces of male, female, young, and old monkeys were projected. The monkeys were confined in a cage and watched these faces go by. When they were released, they made their way toward the screens. Raisins had been placed under the face of one female, a mother, as a reward. The monkeys soon learned to make their way to this "interesting" face. Then this face was replaced by that of one of her offspring. The monkeys very soon found their way to this face, showing that they recognized the link between mother and baby; thus they were capable of perceiving a family resemblance or an affective structure! In this case we are far, indeed very far, from mere physical "stimulation." The monkeys' perception was structured abstractly by a meaning that was already very elaborate. I propose to use the term "perceptive intelligence" to designate this selection and interpretation activity which already marks the reception of sensory stimuli by animals. These stimuli do not consist of "raw" data; here there is no information *per se*.

The best evidence that can be supplied resides in a phenomenon that is widely known today because it was minutely studied by the pioneers of animal ethology. I am speaking of the famous "imprinting," which shows that one and the same piece of information may, depending on the moment of development of the receiving organism, take on a supermarking value or, on the contrary, no value whatsoever.

The simplest and most famous experiment was conducted by Konrad Lorenz, who showed how a duckling can attach to any moving object in its visual field provided it goes by when the duckling is between thirteen and sixteen hours old. In the first thirteen hours after birth, the duckling moves around randomly and is unable to attach to any object. After the seventeenth hour it will attach less and less. But in the intermediate period, which is called the "sensitive period," in ninety percent of cases it will attach to any object that presents itself. The duckling follows the object, and snuggles up to it to sleep; it will never leave it and will only explore its world in the vicinity of "its" object. The object is said to be "imprinted" in the duckling. One can see that it now has a tranquilizing function: the duck becomes familiar with its world by relying on it. Take away the beloved object and the duck will show every sign of stress; it will be distracted and deprived in a purposeless universe. After only a moment it starts to run in all directions; it bumps into things, gets hurt, and stops eating and drinking; it is unable to sleep. Any stimulation only increases its stress.

Today we know that Konrad Lorenz had a stroke of luck, as indeed the duck appears to be the species that takes to imprinting best. However, it has been shown, since the time of this memorable work, that this "sensitive period" is only in fact a maximum receptivity period whose duration can be varied experimentally. If the duckling is isolated it becomes hypersensitive so that it can be imprinted a little before hour thirteen; if it is overstimulated before the sensitive period, it is possible to attenuate the imprinting and prolong it a little past hour seventeen. So the process is not quite as rigid as Lorenz had stated, and yet it is very well defined. You may ask: what is this "object" to which the duckling attaches? Anything! It can be a lamp, another duckling, or even the hand of the ethologist. The experiment has been repeated on kittens and puppies: they too can be imprinted but the duration of the sensitive period is much longer. It has been estimated at about five weeks for dogs to several months for primates. I am not speaking about human beings for now, but I will come back to them.

So ethologists must beware of looking at the animal world as a physical and chemical world; on the contrary, they must attempt, by focused observation and comparison, to pinpoint the meaning that is already circulating through this world. Yet one must avoid falling into the opposite and symmetrical trap, which is far more common, more popular, and more formidable: the anthropomorphic trap that "spontaneously" leads us to interpret animal behavior in human terms.

This flawed thinking is all the more insidious in that it grabs us by one of our best-established weaknesses: the emotion we feel when we perceive another being. Let us take the familiar case of the cat. You see it rub up against objects and undulate lovingly against your leg. How can you fail to be melted by this adorable furry being who shows you so much affection? However, reality has nothing to do with the feelings you project onto it. The little rascal has an olfactory gland on the outer part of its mouth: as it rubs, it marks you with its odor and thus proceeds methodically to construct its familiar world. Once it has been properly marked, this world in which the cat installs you without your knowledge will no longer be fearful to it, and it can live there in safety. So it is not to please you that your kitty comes and rubs up against you; it is very "selfishly" making sure of its own affective comfort!

Here is a more sophisticated experiment which reveals the same trap. A population of puppies is divided into two groups at birth. One group is isolated from the mother and deprived of any affective stimulation, while the others are raised under the usual conditions. In about month three or five, a group of psychologists enters the corridor of the laboratory, whereupon the puppies are released. The psychologists have been told that some of these puppies grew up in an emotionally deprived situation, which is described to them in the appropriate words; then they are asked to identify which group is which. At this point the psychologists are unanimous and they are all wrong: for them, the "well brought up" puppies are the ones that jump up at them to greet them, lick them, and surround them, demonstrating their high-spiritedness, as they see it. On the contrary, however, it is the puppies raised in isolation who jump up at the psychologists to mark them and familiarize the environment which is opening up to them for the first time, while the "properly brought up" pups perceive the newcomers as strangers in a world that has already been familiarized by their mothers. In this case their behavior is ambivalent: they are interested and approach, but fearful and brace themselves with their forepaws. "An asocial posture," say the psychologists blandly!

Why are they wrong? Because they have projected onto the puppies the affective gratification they themselves felt at this joyous greeting! Indeed, breeders understand very well the strength of this misunderstanding. The less scrupulous of them use it to their profit to hook the customer: they isolate the animals in cages from birth, making them systematically sick. Then the customer shows up, is seduced by the enthusiasm directed at him or her, and unhesitatingly carries away a sick animal.

However, anthropomorphism often takes less directly affective paths. There may be cases of unthinking and therefore erroneous analogies, although affectivity is not entirely absent, as we shall see. Let us return to cats, or more precisely, to the well-known licking of newborn kittens by their mother. What could be more moving than the new kitten's first bath? Watching this meticulous, patient care, people go into raptures of emotion. The cat is obviously a good mother, loving and attentive! Unfortunately for this edifying scene, the mother is not "washing" her kitten at all; it is we human beings who have invented the myth that the mother is giving her kitten a bath. Actually, she is marking it with her odor and making it "familiar." Evidence: if she is prevented from licking it as soon as it is born, she treats it as a stranger. Sometimes this excellent mother will even eat the kitten.

An (involuntary?) ethologist's joke: the same observation has been made on the cat's favorite prey, rats, which have the habit of grooming themselves immediately after giving birth. Someone had the ingenious idea of dressing them up in "tutus," not to transform them into ballet dancers, but to block the natural sequence of behavioral events which leads to her babies' first bath: the mother is unable to mark the baby rats with her odor. So she will devour them.

A variation on this experiment: if you plug up the nostrils of a ewe, or smear its baby lamb with an unfamiliar odor, you get the same results. The ewe does not eat the lamb, to be sure, but will consider it a stranger and drive it away with no further ado!

The anthropomorphic illusion not only affects our interpretation of animal behavior: it imprints, so to speak, our own behavior toward animals.

Think for example of the mistakes made by all those who try to photograph or film birds. All that wasted film! They quite simply "forget" that animals' eyes do not face the front, so if they want to look at us they have to turn their heads. If they do happen to look at us face on, it is a sign that they want to run away or attack because they are afraid. If you point the camera at them face on, they will interpret this as aggressive behavior and fly away! Hence the blurred pictures of startled flights, the work of ethologists having a field day (a field full of weeds!) or clumsy tourists.

Other professionals—primatologists, veterinarians, animal tamers, and bullfighters—have made similar observations on the proper behavior toward mammals. When you stare at a dog straight on, for example, you engender in the animal a strong sensation of distrust. The misunderstanding does not stop there: to temper its feelings, the dog draws back its lips slightly and lays its ears back a little. People are quick to interpret this change in the animal's face—veterinarians speak of a dog's "face"—as a kind of smile. Assuming it is a smile, they do not even ask themselves what the smile means: even within the human species, a smile does not mean the same thing in Europe and in Asia; European animal lovers wish a Western smile on their dogs without batting an eyelid!

Misinterpretations are less flagrant and less frequent among the apes, because their musculature, position, and eye movements are closer to those of our own. Still, it is by no means easy to get up close to an ape. Primatologists have taught us that to be admitted into a group of gorillas, you have to sit down; then, if possible, eat something—chew on a blade of grass for example—and look at them only sideways, moving slightly. They know that if you look straight into an ape's eyes it will experience an intolerable feeling close to aggression. I see here further evidence, if further evidence were needed, of the existence of perceptive thinking in animals; in the case of an ape, this thinking is manifested by a sequence of calming mimicries: it will open its mouth, keeping its teeth hidden, crouch, display its rear, or make a food offering with its palms in the air—a propitiation ritual, in fact.

BEAUTY AND THE BEASTS

A few years ago, I had the occasion to make an observation that confirms the results of all this work. I had taken some children into the deer enclosure of a zoo, and had decided to measure the animal's bolting distance and film the scene so that I could run the film in slow motion and find out what had startled the animals into flight. Some children in the group were psychotic. We were surprised to make the following discovery, which was highly mysterious to begin with: the does allowed the psychotic children to come up close to them but were frightened by the normal children! We even saw one little girl with Down syndrome, raised in a psychiatric institution because she had been abandoned, snuggle up to a doe that had allowed her to approach without moving a muscle. The same doe approached by a normal child jumped when the child got within three yards and bolted.

Viewed in slow motion, our film revealed what was going on. The psychotic children, lost in their own inner worlds, avoided looking at the animals, often walked sideways, and moved slowly. The very nature of their disorder made them nonthreatening to the deer. The other children, however, as the film quite clearly showed, looked straight at the deer, smiled at them (thus baring their teeth) and raised their hands to pet them; then they rushed at them with affection and enthusiasm. These are all signs of aggression in the deer world! I had an experience of the same type with two dogs and two children, one of whom was a little "wild" girl born from an incestuous relationship. The "tame" child wanted to play with the dogs and grab the dish from which they were eating. The dogs growled and looked threatening. The child was frightened and backed off—she had gotten the "message." But the little "wild" girl went up close, right into the dogs' corner, lay down, and stole the dish. And the dogs put up with it! Here again, when you play the tape back you see that, unlike her companion, the "wild" girl never looked at the dogs; she crawled along and pushed the dogs by butting their rears with her head, just as puppies do to block the aggressiveness of adult dogs.

This little girl illustrated for us how human ethology could have come about. Life sometimes puts people through terrible natural experiments which we are unable to observe under normal conditions. Although the method of observation is far from being simple or clear, the subject of the signs described in this way is far more stimulating to us clinicians than certain laboratory objects that are too "refined" and too artificial.

Laura is a child of incest. Her paternal grandfather wanted to keep her because he saw her as a love child. Her mother, fifteen years old, bewildered with distress at the time of the birth, did not have the strength to take care of her. Thus the baby survived in a family situation of emotional deprivation. At the age of seven months she had to be hospitalized because she was losing the will to live. The warmth of the nurses and environmental stimuli brought the child back to life. Once she was back in her family, her almost total isolation caused a relapse. Finally, at age seven, she was placed in a foster home.

From that point on, every day she would meet her foster parents, the grandparents, the daughter of the house, two large dogs, three ducks, not to mention pigeons, sparrows, hedgehogs, and all the friends and neighbors who dropped by. One Saturday we visited the child to observe her in the environment in which she normally lived.

Surprise number one: she was crawling or pulling herself along on her bottom. Having been brought up in sensory isolation, she had no model for standing and thus had never grasped the idea of walking on her hind legs. A motor behavior apparently as simple as standing upright still requires a learning model!

Indeed it is a mystery that human beings walk on their hind legs, because it brings about all sorts of complications: varicose veins, hemorrhoids, sciatica, digestive disorders, and blood-pressure fluctuations. In terms of purely anatomical logic, we should be walking on all fours, but in terms of human logic this would be very strange indeed.

The question of origin is always a fascinating one. Who was the first individual to have the idea of standing upright? And why? We may play with hypotheses: one day someone wanted to see into the distance, over the grassy plains. The very choice of this hypothesis implies that our sensory equipment was already working well in the area of vision, but that our sense of smell was performing poorly. If my dog tried walking on his hind legs to see over the grass, his performance would be impaired because his eyes would give him a blurred vision of the world in pastel colors, whereas his nose, a few inches from the ground, presents him with a nice, clear, olfactory "map." He would therefore derive no benefit from walking on his hind legs.

Perhaps the first human to walk wanted to free up his or her hands to carry fruit or tools, or perhaps wanted to make an impression on others in the group who were still on all fours!

These intellectual games about the beginnings of a behavioral pattern may seem commonplace. In fact, they always trigger heated reactions because questions about origins evoke pictures based on religious beliefs and, in this area, any disagreement leads to exclusion.

On the other hand, all parents agree when they describe their babies' first attempt at walking. This first risk-taking endeavor becomes a red-letter day for the family, although this learning experience will lead to any number of bumps and bruises, disappearances, and arguments. Logically, if we want to protect our children, we should forbid them to learn to walk.

Luckily, emotional logic creates a field of affective forces that will mold the behavior of the little one. First, the child tries to stand up: then it gives a push and holds steady for a few seconds before wavering and falling back onto Nature's shock absorber, the buttocks. Evolution has arranged things very nicely since human beings are the only species to have this double cushion. This muscular performance, solitary to begin with, shows that the baby is taking risks and having a grand time, despite the resulting bumps and bruises. This eroticization of pain, this solitary pleasure, this game with fear will be amplified by the emotional reactions from the surrounding adults. At this point, the game of exploring the capacities of its own body becomes an intense emotional pretext for the child. It is as if the child were thinking: "All I have to do is to push myself into a standing position to get a rich accolade of coos and hugs. As soon as they all see me stand up, this motor act becomes an extraordinary relational event."

Of course, this is a thought without words. Rather we should call it an organized representation from the perceptions of the child's own body and the emotions coming from those around it.

This observation, an exceptionally commonplace one, means that when no one else is around, the act of pushing itself up onto its legs remains a motor act and has no relational value. A child without a human setting will never assign a relational function to this act of pushing up. Although perfectly capable of walking, he or she is deprived of the shaping force that comes from other people's feelings, and will never try the feat of walking—a performance that, in this context, has no meaning for the child.

Other children attempt the two-legged adventure laboriously because an absent, depressive, or sick environment does not offer the vital force necessary to inject emotion into this motor act, thus depriving it of meaning. Sometimes it is the child itself that will not dare to attempt this adventure because the little stab of pain is no fun, and so risk-taking causes more fear than pleasure. Such a child is then observed to be afraid of trying different kinds of food, rearranging toys, or exploring the unknown.

Very soon after she was welcomed into her foster home, Laura tried walking on two legs. First she wavered for a long time, walking with her elbows pressed to her body without using her arms to balance, and turning around, even halfway, was perilous for quite a while. When the risk became too scary, she found it more reassuring to "walk" sitting down. But as soon as the affection from her new family stimulated her once again, Laura learned to walk like a human being.

Watching Laura taught me that, while it is undeniable that access to language creates a specifically human universe, it is no less true that, before speech, the human universe has a host of affective adventures in store for us, like the face-to-face encounter of mother and child, or the two-legged learning which molds our buttocks just as speech molds our faces, thus creating the anatomical and affective prerequisites for speech.

A long time ago, animal tamers empirically worked out taming methods that reproduced the "tactics" we have just analyzed. The same is true of bullfighters. When the bull enters the ring, he stops and looks around him. He makes a note of the point where he entered, which is the place where he will feel safest. The bullfighter is aware of this: in order to entice the bull to fight, it will have to be drawn out of this protective zone. Ethology can provide a rational explanation for his know-how. It can even account for a number of accidents attributable to poor positioning of persons in the bull ring.

We have now said quite enough to show why anthropomorphism is to be distrusted as much as, if not more than, anthropocentrism. The animal's world does not at all appear to be a world devoid of meaning: as soon as it responds to a stimulus, the animal escapes, even though only a little, from the rigorous constraints of the surrounding outside world; a minimum "meaning" manifests itself which in certain cases can even be quite elaborate. But this meaning never shows up as a human meaning; if the "given" datum has been well and truly interpreted, it has been interpreted in terms of an animal world which is not governed by the same set of meanings as ours.

As long as we steer clear of these two errors, a new field of questions opens up to investigation: the questions raised today by the new discipline of "human ethology." The point is not, as some might think, to "extrapolate" from animal behavior to human behavior, thus humanizing animals to better animalize humans; rather, on the basis of their greater resemblance, it is to pinpoint the difference that makes human beings a species like no other. Even so, the idea is not to mark a "break"; nor is it to underline a continuum. Human ethology shifts the question and aims to show how the human being, because of speech, gains a new degree of freedom in the building of meaning relative to the immediate constraints imposed by the outside world. All this without losing sight of one important fact: this gain in ideality is possible only with a physical, particularly neurobiological, basis and through the use of other physical and material elements such as sensory perception, gaze, posture, distances, and speech.

II

FINGER POINTING

THE FIRST WORD

Human beings are endowed with speech. This is the main event. What is more, to measure its vast scope, we have to envision it as an event or, if you will, an advent. Ethology brings to this study the contribution of the questions with which it deals and the methods of observation that are peculiar to it. It cooperates with other disciplines: linguistics, ethnology, ethno-linguistics, psychiatry, psychoanalysis, neurobiology, child psychology, and more.

The speed with which children learn to speak in a few short months is simply mind-boggling. We witness a sudden speeding up of a process that has thus far been very slow and apparently chaotic into a veritable explosion of verbal language. Between the twentieth and thirtieth months, without the aid of any school, the child learns words, accents, rules, and even exceptions to rules. No teacher, however gifted, will later be able to elicit such a performance in so little time! Consider that in ten months a child learns several hundred words; what is more, as soon as the words are learned, the child starts to play with them and very soon comes up with puns that can be quite poetic, downright hilarious, or brutally aggressive! Not only does the child understand that the word refers to the thing, but soon discovers that a given word can refer not to the thing directly but to another word that refers to the thing, and that pleasure can be found in this process. The mesmerized adult notices that a twenty-month-old toddler can have a sense of humor and is able quite unselfconsciously to turn the physical constraint of the immediate stimulus into ridicule.

It is worthwhile to ponder carefully this runaway miracle. Its mechanisms became a little clearer to me through an observation of ethology, which took place in several phases. To begin with, it seeks its hypotheses and its questions in animal ethology. When you think about "animal communication," you cannot fail to become interested in the function of "designating" objects. Before it is verbalized, this function is unquestionably manifested by understanding and by the use of pointing. Just try pointing your index finger to show a dog where a coveted piece of meat is to be found: it will come right up to your finger and butt it with its nose. You can point as many times as you like; the dog will become more and more frustrated, but will keep coming back. This can be a family pastime for Sunday afternoon. Do what you may, your dog will never "understand" the designating gesture. The index finger means nothing to your dog; the finger cannot signal to some other thing; it is only a finger signalling back to itself. It takes a lengthy period of training before a carefully selected hunting dog can take off in the direction in which its master points. We see that, without exception, dogs remain subject to the proximity of stimuli, even if they apply the small amount of space and time surrounding them to themselves. They access meaning only if it is immediate, right up close to the biological stimulus.

Now look at the behavior of a chimpanzee. Although it has all the necessary fingers and one might even say a few more than are strictly necessary, it never points a finger. Properly speaking, chimpanzees have no index finger. But does it understand when you point? In most cases the answer must be no; the only known exceptions concern humanized chimpanzees who have been raised in captivity. This is surprising when you think that these same chimpanzees, like gorillas, have shown themselves to be capable of learning sign language. The Gardner husband and wife team in 1971 taught Washoe, a female chimpanzee, a gestural language derived from Ameslan (American Sign Language). In 1975, Ann and David Premack worked out a symbolic language with pieces of colored plastic and were able to teach over a hundred words to a chimpanzee. We are all impressed when we see a gorilla taking someone by the arm and using a veritable code of linguistic signs to communicate! These performances are not intellectually paltry. On the contrary, certain chimpanzees manage almost completely to use the three hundred signs in Ameslan; they even manage to combine these signs to form actual sentences. I believe that many politicians carve out careers for themselves with less than that!

Let us return to finger pointing. The only living being in which this signal appears "spontaneously" is, in actual fact, the little human being who thus evidences greater freedom with respect to the proximity of meaningful stimulation. We decided to study in depth the appearance of this gesture in the course of its ontogenesis. The conclusions we were able to draw concern all the meaningful behaviors of the child, beginning obviously with language acquisition, a process which has been amply studied in the recent past. The names of Henri Wallon and Jean Piaget come to mind; they have made their mark on the history of cognitive psychology; the names of Hubert Montagner and Jacques Cosnier are associated with the first ethologic studies of preverbal communication. Guided by our question, we ourselves systematically made comparisons between children whose development was deemed "normal" and children with major communicative disorders, deprived of access to language as a vehicle for communication.

This is the protocol we set up to observe the appearance of finger pointing in "normal" babies. The baby was put in its high chair with a table in front and out of its reach. On the table was placed an object designated by the mother and coveted by the baby: teddy bear, rag, cookie, etc. Using a camera, we took what we called a "short sampling": a sequence of five minutes every month in the same more or less standardized situation. We found that at the age of nine or ten months, the child restrained in its high chair first stretches all its fingers toward the coveted object, looks at it, then starts to yell when it finds it is unable to reach it; then throws itself back and soon engages in self-aggressive behavior, biting its hands for example. The mother says the child is up to one of its little games. Since we are scientists, we call that "hyperkinesia." Statistically, when we repeat this observation systematically, we find almost no deviation from this pattern.

But all of a sudden, in about the tenth or eleventh month for girls and the thirteenth or fifteenth for boys, we see a behavioral change that can easily be seen on the film. Because of its neurological maturity, the child stops holding out its hand with the fingers spread. The event occurs: it starts pointing. This is progress of great significance, because to make this gesture the child must have a fully organized thought: it must stop wanting to grab the object; it must acquire the highly elaborate representation of referring to something which is far away in space and which it can obtain through the intermediary of its mother by designating it.

A more detailed analysis of the film in our sequence invariably shows a "detail" which passes virtually unobserved in "real life" with the naked eye, but whose importance proves to be decisive. When it makes its designating gesture, the child looks at the mother or the father or other adult in the room. We say that it is turning to what we call, in our terminology, its "attachment figure." It is then, at this precise moment, that the child attempts, invariably failing at first, to articulate a word. I have ventured to coin a word to designate this failed word: I call it a "proto-word"; we perceive it as an acoustic emission sounding like "bah-bah."

We will be looking later at some other teaching derived from this observation. For the time being we will content ourselves with spotlighting this one fact: language begins to appear only on the basis of a designative behavioral cluster that assumes a given degree of biological maturity and takes place not when the child is face to face with the thing it designates but with the aid of a dual affective reference to the thing and the person of attachment. Thus a thing can become a designated "object" and the theme of a vocalization which regularly accompanies pointing. On this point we share the conclusions of A. Jouanjean l'Antoene, who studied this gesture in a day-care center and believes that it "leads us to the beginnings of symbolism and the origins of the ability to evoke absent objects."

AUTISTIC CHILDREN AND "CLOSET" CHILDREN

Other observations, this time from the field of clinical and even psychiatric ethology, will allow us to confirm and enrich these initial results. Here we use the same methods to observe children who do not have access to language, as a result of accidents or diseases such as meningitis. These encephalopathic children have an intact genetic competence identical to that of all children, but their brains are damaged and the apparatus that perceives the world is deformed. They do not live in the same sensory universe as we do; unable to process information like other people, they select different perceptions and organize them according to other modalities. While, like us, they live with the facts of the world that is given to them, this world is not ours. And, we find that these children

THE DAWN OF MEANING

never reach the pointing stage! They remain at the stage of hoarse yells with hands extended and fingers spread toward the coveted object; the hyperkinesia and self-aggression persist. Let us not hasten, however, to conclude that they "stay at this level"; this would assume "arrested development." In reality it is their world; a stable world with which they are grappling, as we do with ours. Their behavior is not in the least fixed and congealed; it is able to develop like any human behavior but develops on a different basis and along other directions.

This immediately proves that access to language assumes "ethologic prerequisites" (J. Cosnier). But these prerequisites, while they appear to be necessary conditions, absolutely cannot be held to be sufficient conditions.

Observation of autistic and abandoned children allows us to understand this readily. While they have the same neurological equipment as all other children, they do not point with their fingers; in scientific terminology, they have the same "behavioral ontogenesis" as encephalopaths. Let us consider the tragic case of the abandoned children known in France as "closet children." The expression in all its cruel realism designates the increasingly widespread phenomenon euphemistically termed "abandoned at home" by social workers. Alone all day long, these children are shut up by their parents in a small room "to protect them" or "prevent them from doing something silly." They wait there, prisoners, the entire day for the return of the adults who are off somewhere attending to their own affairs. I have seen even more terrible cases, like that of a little boy whose parents chained him to his bed before going off for a week-end of skiing in the mountains. The unfortunate child went all day without eating or drinking, lying in his own urine. When his parents returned, they washed him, fed him, hugged and kissed him with an apparently clear conscience!

This example shows that this type of behavior is sometimes manifested in the well-to-do social classes. It turns out that such "closet children" who live all day in a state of social and sensory deprivation never learn to point. This shows that not only are there neurological prerequisites for opening the door to language, but there are also affective prerequisites! The behavioral system which "supports" speech and brings it about assumes the presence around the child of some other being to talk to and to talk for; speech must be answered by some other speech. This person, whoever it may be, is required for the child to venture into signs and speech. Failing such a person, the door will remain closed. Is this closure definitive? One moving case which is on record allows us to say that it is not. It involves a psychotic boy aged five. The protocol went as follows. There was a hut, and the mother had put the child's teddy bear out of his reach on the roof of the hut. The boy went toward the teddy bear, stretched out his fingers, and started to yell. When we ran the film in slow motion, I and my fellow workers noticed that, in the middle of his cries, the child took a furtive look at his mother and began to make the ghost of a pointing gesture. We ran the film in slow motion to the educators and doctors who were caring for this child. We took the risk of affirming that, if our theory was correct, this child was "depsychotizable," since he had furtively manifested the behavioral cluster necessary to attempt an affective and social relationship. Thus, we did not feel that the mental prison was shut tight.

Indeed, this child is no longer psychotic today. Was this cure attributable to our intervention? I would not be so bold as to assert it; all I know is that this little boy was very kind to our theory.

We may wonder what is the future of closet children reintroduced to speech. They usually retain traces of the initial affective deprivation. In little boys, this is manifested in an insatiable desire to make the mother love them and to "seduce" her. When they grow up, they make every effort to gain this affection that was not given to them as children. This leads to severe conflicts with their wives when the women discover that their mothers-in-law are invincible and "devouring" rivals! The "logic" of this behavior of absolute devotion seems to be very simple: "She didn't love me because I didn't deserve her love. I will now live by sacrifice and give so much of myself that she will have to love me in the end." Perhaps here is the origin of masochism.

The dawn of meaning and its expression in speech are so much governed by affective relationships that it is appropriate to observe the genesis of this relational cluster. When we do so, we find that this genesis starts in a "word bath," to borrow an expression from Françoise Dolto.

Let us trace the life of a child back to its earliest days. One observation I made in day-care centers showed me precisely the role of speech in the development of newborn infants. I recorded the crying of premature infants and of newborn infants. When I took my tapes to the frequency analyzer, I was able to see the babies' cries converted into sound images. The analyzer printed out a sort of histogram or bar chart which, on photographic paper, showed the distribution of low and high frequencies from left to right. I could see that if the babies were left together they made "square" cries and answered each other from cradle to cradle with such square cries. All this is rhapsodic, not to say cacophonic. If, on the other hand, they are in a setting where adults are talking around them, starting on the fourth day the crying takes on a melodic line and when they answer each other back they compose a sort of cradle symphony!

Hence it appears that adult speech represents highly meaningful information for these newborns, to which they respond by modulating their cries.

This upsets quite a number of preconceived notions. We are forced to admit that babies not only perceive sounds as soon as they are born but that they also recognize sounds, that is they differentiate between different sonorities. Just as we have to shed our anthropomorphism to observe animals, it is urgently necessary for us to get rid of our arrogant adultomorphism if we want to understand the world of babies. This is because babies do not content themselves with reacting differently to the crying of other babies and the speech of adults. We see that, in a stable setting, their cries are enriched with low frequencies. But if someone enters, perhaps a nurse coming in to change the bedding, high frequencies will be more numerous in the next set of cries! Their expression of sounds proves to be highly discriminating.

If we now do the experiment of playing recordings of baby cries rich in high frequencies to animals, you will see that dogs, for example, start to whimper and cats meow with anxiety. If you play the tape to adults you will immediately trigger anxious somatizations. "I feel ill," say women. "This crying gives me a stomach ache." The wife of one of my friends told me she couldn't tolerate it and it made her feel awful, without being able to state exactly what she felt.

The virulence of these reactions was all the more striking and even enlightening in that it followed on the heels of highly neutral and even detached comments when the same people listened to low-frequency cries: "Hey, it's a boy... He must be hungry! He reminds me of my son!"

What are we to conclude from these observations if not that babies, as soon as they are born, familiarize a world into which colors and smells, as well as sounds and especially words, enter as essential elements; that a human child, far from passively bowing to the law of the environment, introduces a certain order to it and a series of differences to which it reacts?

Adults never tire of interpreting these reactions according to markers of their own adult world. "She's fretting," or "he's anxious," we say of a newborn baby. But these are only markers that we believe we can read from the child's body and that we relate to our own experience of anxiety and what it does to our own bodies. Careful, now: let us not speak of anxiety because the world of the newborn is a world in which no words are exchanged. Let us say that the signs we interpret as markers of anxiety are caused by the infant's unfamiliarity with its environment. This will prevent us from constructing psychological novels, particularly about birth and the famous supposed "birth trauma." These only express the point of view of adults who project their own anxieties into the interpretation they apply to the newborn. In fact, at the time of birth, the baby is sound asleep—only in stage three or light sleep. This thought probably troubles us because we say that a baby "sees the light of day" when it is born. And yet it is asleep. This has consistently been verified by encephalography. The "birth trauma" dear to Otto Rank (1884–1939) thus appears to be a figment of Rank's imagination, and of the imaginations of those who followed him. During the next hour, this newborn infant, fast asleep, has familiarized itself with the sensory information it already began to perceive at the end of the pregnancy. Delivery appears to be a "change of environmental scene" and perhaps that is what constitutes birth trauma: the baby passes from a world of water to a world of air and finds in this world information that is already familiar to it, although modified.

THE ONTOGENESIS OF THE MUG

Today we have observational and recording tools that allow us to look inside the uterus before birth and monitor the fetus' marvelous process of familiarization with the world, and thus reestablish a continuity between intrauterine life and the new familiarization out in the open. Alexandre Minkowski proposes to call this field "fetal ecology." I will briefly run through a few items of observation that deal with the dawn of meaning. When the mother speaks, the fetus perceives the low frequencies from her speech as filtered through the chest, the diaphragm, and the uterus. As perceived by the unborn baby, the mother's voice is remote, soft, and low (the sonority has been analyzed by computer). But the voices of others who live with the mother—the father for example— also reach the fetus. The sound has to pass through only a thin wall of muscle and water to reach its internal ear, so the fetus perceives the voice as being higher and shriller. Studies show that the frequencies of this voice are exactly superimposed on those of the noises of the uterus, so that the unborn child will have distinguished only the mother's voice. On the other hand, it is possible that the odor of the father is perceived by the fetus, as molecules inhaled by the mother have been found in the amniotic fluid at the end of pregnancy. We should also bear in mind the observations by Frans Veldman: when the father places his hands on the mother's abdomen during the two months preceding birth, the fetus changes position. Gynecologists have been using this maneuver for a long time when the intrauterine position of the unborn child has to be changed.

Between the very first days and the "critical" moment of "finger pointing," when the child acquires an "index finger," months go by during which new elements of the "meaningful" behavioral system peculiar to the young of human beings are set in place. One of the most striking and most universal episodes contributing to the organization of this system and to stabilization of the child's world is the choice of a "pacifying object." Today it is observed that few children are able to do without this: the choice may fall on a teddy bear or a handkerchief, but it may also be an older brother or sister, a familiar noise—the sound of the television, for example, or even of the father clearing his throat in the next room. In all cases it will be a sensory, visual, or acoustic object, that may or may not be obvious at first glance, to which the child attributes a familiarity function. It may be said that no human being can live without satisfying this "teddy bear function." In more scientific terms, we say that every human being takes up an "object of attachment" to help assemble his or her world and explore the universe. I spoke of "episode," but we all know that this phase may last for some time. The teddy bear function continues until well after the advent of language. The child usually does not detach from it until he or she goes off to school. It is not possible to provide a complete picture of the process of formation of this world of "objects" endowed with meaning, a process to which every human being, generation after generation harnesses himself or herself with terror and with delight. I will, however, note one more feature, a decisive element in the history of human beings: the making of tools. Here, again, we may be guided by observations in human ethology.

We know that in a natural environment certain animals are capable of making tools: monkeys can take a branch and use it as a fishing rod. They also manufacture and use sponges and adopt what might be termed "sponge behavior." After a rain, water is caught in tree trunks. But drinking this water is far from straightforward because the mouth cannot get into the hollows and crevices. So monkeys dip their fingers and suck them, but very quickly tire of this procedure. They then pick up leaves, chew them, stuff them into the trunk, wait a little while, then take them out and drink the water they have absorbed. Then they start all over again.

People have often doubted that animals have the ability to invent tools. Here is one example. It is all the more striking that controlled time management is involved. The monkey perceives the leaves, imagines that chewed leaves could be inserted into the trunk to soak up water, and "knows" that water can be drunk from the sponge. Better still, it waits for the leaves to become thoroughly soaked before withdrawing them and conveying them to its mouth. We may measure the ability to chain representations implied by this procedure. Whatever epistemologists may say, the monkeys give them the lie: here we have "intelligence" or perceptive "thought."

Now imagine two little girls looking at a mug. One of them is a familiarized child aged three and a half; the other a "wild child," abandoned at an early age, and seven years old. The first child, turning up for her afternoon snack, goes through a linked sequence of gestures: she picks up the mug, drinks the contents, looks at her mother, and puts the mug down again. The wild little girl picks up the mug, drinks, and as soon as her thirst is quenched, opens her hand and lets the mug drop.

Both little girls have perceived the mug and have understood that it is not a thing but a tool that can be filled with water; they take the tool as such and both know how to use it. But the wild girl stops right there, while the familiarized little girl continues the ontogenesis of the object. Here, as in the case of finger pointing, we have discovered the crucial detail: looking at the mother (or the adult present). The little girl is addressing herself to her mother's affectionate gaze at the same time as she is handling the object. The object is thus socialized. When there is speech, the mother will say or will have said: "You know, your Aunt Mary gave you that mug for your christening." So by looking at her daughter she "historicizes" the object; it becomes permeated with a background and a religion. The substance of the "mug object," like that of my Louis XIII armoire, is made up of meaning and woven with words; this is why it is human.

Let us recapitulate this "ontogenesis of the mug": the first stage is that of the "thing" (drinking-leaves). Then comes the thing thought of as a tool, the object of a perception-representation. All children have access to this way of thinking; but the familiarized little girl adds the socialization to this "object" which for her becomes part of the family. Closet children, on the other hand, demonstrate the decisive nature of this socialization for the becoming-human of human children: for them, objects remain things. They just about make it to the status of tools, but never become "meaningful" objects.

III

OBJECTS OF

ATTACHMENT

THE TEDDY BEAR FUNCTION

We have seen how, from animals to humans, meaning is imparted to the thing and transforms it into an object. For humans, meaning becomes detached from the immediate biological or technical environment; borne by words, humans play a game with themselves according to specific but open rules which open up to them a vista whose only horizon is infinity.

My dog already lives in an order of meanings; he manages to deal with an elementary class of signs. But to respond to a sign and insert it into his scheme of things, he needs perceptions that are close in space and confined to a short period of time.

As for me, however, I have no difficulty in accommodating my wife's entire family inside my Louis XIII armoire. I live in an order of signs that might be called a "higher" order: the symbol penetrates the sign and gives wing to my thoughts that can fly far further than the admirable butterfly; in an instant it delves into the 16th century and settles down to look for the ancestors of my armoire.

However, there is one feature of "our" world that I have not yet discussed and which should put a stop forever to our speaking, as we so casually but so regularly do, of the "animal nature of human beings." This feature, which for a long time went unnoticed, unrecognized, or was denied, has been thrust into full relief by our ethologic perspective: speech modifies the very biology of the human being.

Let us return to our "objects of attachment," our teddy bears and our handkerchiefs. Here is a very simple experiment that was set up in the institution where I was working a few years ago. We decided to photograph the objects arranged around the beds of the patients (female patients in this case), then photographed them after they had been "tidied up" by the patients. We noticed that each woman organized her personal space differently according to the type of pathology with which she was afflicted. The arrangement of objects always has a specific significance. One woman would place seven children's photos above the head of her bed, but not a single one represented her own children. This behavior is significantly rooted in her anguished history. Depressed patients get rid of everything in their rooms while, conversely, manics clutter them up with various decorations. When they get depressed, this intense orna-

OBJECTS OF ATTACHMENT

mental activity ceases: no objects to show means
nothing to say; the melancholic or depressed patient
no longer has the strength to speak. In the eyes of
schizophrenics, objects appear to be sorts of "semantic debris." Like the wild children, they perceive and
use objects but do not endow them with social meaning. We see in our photos amazing stacks of maga-
zines, cigarette butts, underpants, cigarette butts in
the underpants, cookies, tumblers—all out of place
and left there as the day wears on.

Speech confers a semantic value on sensory
space; the human "territory" never appears as a space
simply marked as animals mark it, but truly a
"semantic territory" from which "objects" are essentially absent in their very presence since it is
signifiers that matter. Any extrapolation of an animal's "territory" to that of a human being is thus
based on a misinterpretation which has forgotten the
specifically human reality of meaning. But while
sensory space is organized in this way and imbued
with value as a function of affectivity, it feeds back
to the perception, affectivity, and physiology of the
individual; for this reason it is not wrong to say that
on occasion it may be good for patients to experience
a change of scenery and leave the "familiar" place
where they are surrounded by their sickness.

Once more, smell will serve us as a guide; not
analysis of the olfactory molecule but the study of

the behaviors induced by smell, which is not the same thing at all unless we imagine that the cause of an action can be quite simply attributed to a chemical. Molecularistic representation is too often used to avoid thinking: "He's sad because his brain is secreting less dopamine." This overdone effort at explanation dead-ends thinking. Neurologists use molecules to come up with some pretty far-out problems: "Introduction of acetylcholine modifies the representation of the world." The circulation of information between the laboratory and human culture is backwards. But this is pure intellectual laziness, because many aspects of this action, as long as it is not simple mechanical feedback but significant behavior, fall outside this pseudo-explanatory scheme of things.

I will return to the study I recently conducted on handkerchiefs as pacifiers to learn yet another lesson. Using our methods of observation, let us examine the postures of a baby as a function of the olfactory atmosphere. Put the baby into the arms of its mother, then into the arms of another woman, and finally into the arms of a man. In its mother's arms, the baby will immediately calm down; once it is comforted, it will start to observe the outside world. While anxious babies are restless and make disorderly movements in all directions, soothed babies cling to their mothers at the collarbone; once its nose is embedded in the hollow above the collarbone, the

child starts gazing around. This behavior is analo-
gous to that observed in the duckling at the time of
imprinting: it is when the duckling is made to feel
secure by its imprinting object that it becomes
capable of observing and conquering its world.

But in the present case, people will say: how do
we know that this behavior is linked to smell and not
to the baby's position or some other factor we may
not have thought of? I was able to set up an experiment whose results were immediately put to good
use by pediatricians.

I asked a group of mothers to choose two or
three personal objects and present them to their
babies, saying that they were indeed objects belong-
ing to mother. Each baby "chose" one of these
objects; it manifested a preference for one of them. I
then asked each mother to carry this object in her bra
for two days so that it would be marked with her
smell, then give it to her baby at its bedtime, telling it
once again, and making it quite clear that this object
belonged to its mother and that she had worn it.

All the mothers told me the same story: the
baby took the handkerchief, rubbed it against its
nose, and went right off to sleep. This simple
ethologic observation made it possible to avoid the
use of sleeping medications such as nembutal or
theralene, which had previously been given to
generations of babies that would have been far better
off without them. Nowadays you will see in oper-

ating rooms teddy bears or handkerchiefs clutched to the faces of young surgical patients (who still need anesthesia, however).

The reader will have noted that my protocol prescribed a whole verbal scenario; the child had to be told: "These objects belong to me, choose one; I wore it and it belongs to you."

Several mothers did not fully follow the protocol—this always happens when you're a clinician! They took an object and wore it without telling the child; then they placed it under the baby's nose. The result was the same. I am thankful to these "disobedient mothers," because I have now drawn the conclusion that it is the sense of smell that plays the determinant role.

Since then I've been told a number of stories that confirm, sometimes quite amazingly, the correctness of this interpretation. I came across the case of one little girl, whose parents were both doctors and who suffered from very severe school phobia: the panic attacks she went through when she was sent off to school were fearful to behold. Her mother tried my method even though the child was older than my usual babies. She gave her one of her scarves (imprinted) and watched the little girl go off to school with the scarf. When the child entered the classroom, she placed her scarf in her school bag; when she felt uneasy, she took it out and pressed it to her nose. Her panic attacks went away. Indirectly, I had invented the "pacifier scarf"! The little girl was seen to organize an actual pacification ritual around it, which lasted for quite a while; this ritual was based on smell, but smell insofar as the odor made a "sign" to her mother. During the trip to school the smell of the scarf was the materialized presence of her mother; the link was maintained during her absence: a confirmed attachment despite distance, an affective victory over the threat of space and time. We can now see how useless it is to invoke molecules against meaning, as many persist in doing today. It is quite apparent that the molecule is the bearer of meaning; it is impossible to ignore this meaning when we are trying to explain the role of the molecule in human behavior. In other words, it is the process of familiarization—its history, its successes, and its reverses—which is supported, embodied, and "mediatized" by the olfactory molecule that produces a tranquilizing effect.

One more observation will confirm and refine what I will present as a thesis, because by presenting it I am opposing many others.

Sometimes fathers are the primary caregivers of their children. In these cases, when I asked the mothers to carry an object and present it to the child, the effect was nil. I then asked a father who had nurtured his child during its first few months to test my protocol. The child in this case chose his father's cap, which he gave him, and the little boy went to sleep clutching it to his face. The mother then remarked that this cap, although it helped the little boy to drop off to sleep, disturbed him during the night. The child found the solution all by himself: he had them cut off the cap's stiff visor and keep only the soft part covering the head! To us ethologists, he simply converted the cap into a "pacifying handkerchief"; he had the good taste to come up with our experimental protocol! Once again we see that the olfactory molecule is certainly involved, but as a molecule imbued with meaning. No special chemistry (should I say: no alchemy?) links the child to the mother, since in certain situations the father's molecules can do the same job provided they have been familiarized; thus matter can "sign."

THE SMELL OF THE OTHER

In human beings, smell is a very special sense. On the one hand, hearing is a noble sense because it gives access to speech and music. Vision is acceptable because it leads to pictures. Touch is necessary because it allows us to avoid danger and tells us about pain. All these sensory channels are thus morally tolerated in our condition as humans made of matter.

Smell, on the other hand, which brings us close to my dog and classifies us among the osmatic mammals, triggers in us a feeling of distaste, even shame. We don't want it to become known that we are "descended from monkeys" and that we like to sniff odors that we are ashamed to acknowledge!

How are we to explain this taboo against smell, the feeling of discomfort and affective reactions, of almost erotic relish or virtuous indignation that this sense awakens in us when we speak of it?

The sense of smell is strongly "moralized," as sexuality has always been, just as dreams have been acculturated. Certain cultures, like that of the ancient Greeks or the African Mossi of today, give dreams the power to access a hidden, immaterial private world that is not perceptible in the waking state and even less so during sleep. The Greek or Mossi dream allows us to enter a third world, that of the immaterial and yet quite real psychic world. Our culture has turned dreaming into a biologic and electrophysiologic study with exciting results, while others make it the "royal road to the unconscious." For a long time the interpretation of dreams was forbidden, like palmistry! This is the point at which we stand with smell. Its scientific study is not actually forbidden, but it is not exactly recommended. Like sexuality, like dreams, it is still a part of the shameful side of Western culture: human matter.

Nonetheless, we have tried to observe it, even in adults, and have gone from one surprise to another.

The feeling of intimacy that any study of human smell arouses can be explained by actual penetration; a molecule secreted by the body of another person penetrating into mine, through my nose, where it gives off a pulse of pleasure or rejection. This olfactory pathway does seem to have some similarity to the sexual! Freud and his friend Fliess, a great nose specialist, had foreseen this emotional closeness between sex and nose, but they had made of it a naive theory that was accepted by our culture, amazingly enough because it speaks of the organic "repression" necessary for establishing a civilizing process. The great Jacques Lacan prolonged this ethic of olfactory repression by saying (in his seminar on identification) that "the organic repression of the sense of smell counts for much in its access to the dimension of the Other." Wonderful! What remains in us of the olfactory mammal is crushed to provide some extra humanity. Indeed!

Olfactory racism is an ancient Western value; Voltaire said that he could easily recognize Jews by their bad smell; today it is still common in some languages to insult people by saying that they stink or that one "cannot smell them," meaning "cannot bear them." In sum, subhumans have a bad smell and only those who hold their noses sufficiently high in the air escape the animal in them.

Yet, ethnologists have taught us the degree to which smell participates in social exchanges; but they also show that smells must be coded and ritualized, like sexuality, eating, and sleeping. Everything that goes into making our human condition inevitably physical has to undergo this treatment: it must be impregnated with meaning to form a human condition that escapes physical matter. This is why in New Guinea it is good manners to pass your hand under the armpit of someone you are leaving behind and pass your fingers under your nose to signify that you will treasure the smell of the far-off friend. One can also place one's hand on the *mons veneris* of an esteemed woman; it should be pointed out, however, that these good manners are not universal.

Yet Montaigne thoroughly understood this New Guinea ritual when he explained: "[My] moustaches, which are full, serve (odors) to me. The hard kisses of youth, savory, greedy, and sticky, once clung to them and dwelt there for many an hour." (*Essays*, Book 1, Chapter LV). Michel Serres reminds us that odors have for a long time been part of medical symptomatology: the smells of a pippin apple, acetone, and rotten eggs were taught to me and I have even been told of the smell of schizophrenics!

Once we were aware of the neurological organization of the olfactory circuits in the brain and had been trained in ethologic methods of observation, we attempted to observe what happened when adults were made to smell a battery of odors.

The olfactory nerve endings that perceive the molecule and carry this information to our brain follow a particular route. They do not pause at the "information screening station" of the thalamic nucleus, which channels this information to a specialized zone of the cortex where a representation is created. On the contrary, this smell information passes directly from the nose to the memory and emotion circuits, with no neocortical representation.

What this means is that our brain is organized in such a way that when an odor is perceived, it awakens a diffuse impression, shaped by a memory. Babies already operate with olfactory familiarity, which constitutes a type of short-term memory. Human adults use the nose to awaken an impression and evoke the past scene that corresponds most closely to it.

Olfactometry, the measurement of smell, is a difficult art because the signal is invisible and evaporates very quickly; notwithstanding this, we are all capable of smelling odors and differentiating them. We have been able to focus odor puffs by using some aluminum dishes and small spray bottles.

First surprise: the wealth of the odors that have no name (about 1500 of them and perhaps more).

Second surprise: instant triggering of emotions labeled pleasant or unpleasant.

Third surprise: very rapid evocation of memories and images; as soon as people breathe in a smell, they will tell you an intimate story.

Overall, odors that are called "good" evoke stories of food or of nature: childhood snacks, new-mown hay during vacations, candy stolen from the kitchen, nights lying awake in the countryside, and so forth.

Smells that are called "bad" evoke stories of sickness or civilization: the smell of vomit, of surgery, of stale tobacco (which smokers do not smell because their olfactory nerves have been fried), burnt rubber, and garbage dumps.

This never happens with auditory, visual, or tactile stimulation. The sorting done by the thalamus and routing to a specialized zone of the cortex gives us an almost immediate representation of a word, a piece of music, a picture, a caress, or a burn.

With those sensory channels, we adapt to the present moment, while odor evokes a moment in the past and triggers an emotion.

The ethology of smell clarifies Freud's idea of "the mnesic trace of representations"; it accounts scientifically for the virtues of Proust's madeleine: repetition of the actual pleasure weaves an attachment and its evocation awakens nostalgia.

We are now able to understand better why smell, which lights up the circuits of a third of the brain and is associated with all representations, has such a bad reputation: it is a direct penetration which evokes everything in our intimate lives that is deliciously murky.

The reader may now reproach me for not having demonstrated how speech modifies human biology! You will have noticed it, however. Let us remember the pointing with the finger and continue the analysis up to the moment when the child can pronounce the word that designates the thing at the same time as he or she is pointing to it. It has been shown that, with the disappearance of hyperkinesia and self-aggression, there follows a change in relationships and a maturing of the nervous system. It has been noted that this event is linked to the ability acquired by the child at this same age to stand upright and coordinate all its gestures.

The "teddy bear" function is still more enlightening on this point: children who drop off to sleep fairly easily, pacified by their objects of attachment, structure their sleep more precociously and more harmoniously than those who find it hard to fall asleep, or even those for whom sleeping medications are prescribed. As a result, not only the development of the mental faculties of these children, particularly memory, but also their growth, via the growth hormone, are affected.

THE FIRST SMILE

But there is one observation which, better than any other, shows the "semanticization" of biology by human speech: that of the newborn baby's first smile. We made a project of filming this first smile. We set up a movie camera in the delivery room and turned it on. At the same time we made an electroencephalogram of the baby. Using the film record, we were able to follow the expressions and gestures of the infant at the same time as the changes in its brain waves. This is what happened: the baby slept and its eyes were shut. Suddenly there appeared what we call a smile! If we look at what is happening on the encephalogram we see that the baby has just entered the phase known as "paradoxical sleep." This is the only time the smile appears, like a cerebral alert. Present-day sleep research provides even more information: the first "smile" is determined by a bioelectric secretion of a neuropeptide in the brain.

It's not easy to imagine a mother going into transports of ecstasy before her infant and exclaiming: "Look! Our baby just secreted a neuropeptide!" The mother sees a smile and interprets the facial expression as a smile. We have to say brutally that she is quite wrong—and the consequences of this initial misinterpretation are considerable. Touched and rejoicing, she in turn wants to manifest her tenderness. She goes up to the baby, cradles it in her arms, and kisses it; creating around the infant a sensory world of warmth, smell, and vocal proximity. Result: she stimulates the baby's famous growth hormone! We can pinpoint this on our encephalogram because we know that stage three, which prepares for paradoxical sleep, is the light stage which stimulates the base of the brain and triggers the secretion of this hormone. In this way we can now account for affective "dwarfism": tiny children with spindly limbs and no clear sexual differentiation in their physiognomy.

Conclusion: in this case, our spontaneous adultomorphism turns out to have splendid practical results. By giving a meaning, even a wrong meaning, to the baby's muscular contraction, a parent can change the biological rhythm of its development! From the very first moment, human biology is shaped by speech! Depressive parents furnish a counterexample which unfortunately is far from rare. We know that many women suffer from a depressive episode after labor (scientifically known as "postpartum depression"). It is estimated that as many as one out of four women experience this.

When we make an observation of this type in such cases, we see the baby smile and the mother remain as still as a statue. When she is questioned, she will tell you that she's not allowing herself to make any gesture toward the baby. And you hear these terrible words: "I should never have brought her into the world." "I regret having had a baby, with everything that's out there facing him...." This is how they express their intolerable anguish but, by their failure to react to the smile, they are creating around the baby what I call a "cold sensory world": no facial expression, no odor, and no contact. Thus the ontogenesis of sleep becomes more difficult and the growth of the child will be retarded.

What applies to the growth of children also applies to sexual differentiation between little boys and little girls. In the same way, we see meaning being introduced into their very biology right at the time of birth. If, using our methods, you watch mothers giving babies their first bath, you will see that they do not hold male and female babies in the same way. It has even been possible to draw maps, or atlases if you will, showing the frequency of bodily contact between mother and baby according to certain parts of its body. You can see that a true sexual shaping of the baby's behavior is taking place from the very start: the boy will regularly be held by his shoulders and his abdomen will rarely be touched. The girl is usually held by her bottom and her abdomen is stroked! The ethnologist Hélène Stork made some quite astonishing comparisons of bodily contacts between mother and child, observed in Africa and Asia. She found that there was the same sexualization of the holding gesture, but that instead of being "spontaneous" and implicit as in the Western world, it was often prescribed by the culture she was observing.

It has also been shown that the smile is sexualized: baby girls smile more than baby boys because their parents smile at them more. One need only observe a school class to see the effectiveness of this early child sexualization: little boys and little girls are socialized early on by very different codes. The sexual shaping of the little one's behavior has succeeded; it corresponds exactly to the image adult society has of the role it assigns to each of the sexes. Babies are thus imprinted with cultural coding as soon as they come into the world!

Are we able to say, on the basis of such observations, that human behavior is subject to a sort of destiny driven by biological, semiological, and linguistic elements? When we were talking about the access to speech of the "closet children," we already noted that no isolated determinism was actually at work. This judgment can be refined by another very different example. I am speaking of what we call "post-move depression," which affects people in the thirty to fifty age bracket who suddenly fall into deep depression on the occasion of a normal move; or more frequently they are elderly people who have spent their active lives in the city and want to retire to the country, to the sun. How many of them go into a depression at the very time when they finally realize this dream—a dream for which they have sacrificed a great deal. After the age of seventy or so, such depressions can have a fatal outcome. Doctors on the Riviera, for example, are quite familiar with these innumerable cases of anaclitism[*] in the elderly that are unknown to their Parisian colleagues. Fortunately, although these cases are not uncommon, they are not the rule. It is definitely possible to move without becoming depressed. So how are we to account for these singular depressions? In all the cases we were able to analyze, we discovered the "imprint" of an earlier wrenching experience which left its mark. For a long time it lay dormant, but was reactivated by the move with more or less devastating consequences.

Thus it is that we see people who have, as the saying goes, "everything they could wish to make them happy," (I always add: "except happiness!") lapse into a severe depression. They are afraid to talk about it and allow themselves to die because the apparent cause—leaving their apartment in the city—seems ridiculous! But they are wrong about

---

[*] Anaclitism: a term first used to translate Freud's *Anlehnung*, which refers to the concept of "deprivation of support." Currently used to describe a developing affective pathology: removal of an attachment which deprives the person who depended on it as a basis for security: "I have no one I can count on."

the "cause." When they are questioned, we discover that they were hospitalized in childhood and so had already been—on at least one occasion often deeply buried in their memory—in a state of anaclitism. There remained from these long-gone times a trace of vulnerability at the root of their being, which had become buried with the years; the move reactivated the pain deep in the memory.

Therapeutic conclusions can be drawn from this observation. The first is that one should not be content to prescribe vitamins when a patient in such a situation comes in for consultation. Certainly the person speaks of being "tired" or "fatigued," but obviously vitamins will be of no avail. The second is to discourage the elderly from moving. If the move is inevitable, the person and the family should be warned of what may happen, so that all may be prepared to deal with the situation.

From this set of observations there are also theoretical lessons to be learned about the methodology of human ethology and philosophy which inspires and reinforces these observations.

IV

FREEDOM THROUGH

SPEECH

NATURE NURTURED

For decades, psychologists have been divided over the issue of whether this or that human behavior must be considered "innate" or "acquired." This "nature or nurture" dispute raged fiercely in the discussion of the use of intelligence tests and the measurement of the famous "IQ." Are we measuring innate or even hereditary aptitudes or, as some people have convincingly maintained, a more or less successful adjustment to Western educational standards?

I feel that one of the major benefits of the ethologic approach to human behavior is that we can dodge these huge pseudoconcepts and show that they represent a bogus issue. Eysenck believed that human behavior is 80 percent innate and 20 percent acquired. On the basis of our experience, I would be quite prepared to say that it is 100 percent innate and 100 percent acquired. Or, what amounts to the same thing, nothing is "innate" and nothing is "acquired." We have just discussed numerous examples of this: the acquired can only be acquired by means of the innate, which in turn is always shaped by the acquired. Nature is nurtured!

In actual fact, something which is presented as a discussion, each side of which is based on scientific observation, appears to us to be an avatar of the ancient Western dichotomy, theologized and philosophized, between the body and the soul. The partisans of the soul are indefatigably opposed to the partisans of the body. The words may change—we speak of organogenesis, psychogenesis, etc.—but the old divergence remains. To show how in actual fact this is only an ideological debate dressed up in scientific garb, I took the occasion of the 1974 French presidential elections to do a little experiment: we were having the umpteenth National Scientific Research Center seminar on the innate and the acquired. As usual, the opposite camps were arguing excitedly. I wanted to find out how the votes of the two schools—the proponents of (genetic) innateness of behavior and those of the acquired— were distributed. My colleagues were kind enough to respond to my little survey, and I found that almost all the "nature" people were going to vote for Giscard d'Estaing, the right-wing candidate, while the "nurture" people would vote for Mitterrand, the socialist! This exercise bears repeating more often;

it shows that there are indeed two "world views," two clashing pictures of our species. And this is why there is no way such a debate can be resolved scientifically. If you believe that nature predominates, it means you believe that humankind is subject to the laws of the Universe, in this case the law of chromosomes. And since there is some inequality among people, you will account for it by the inequality of their chromosomes. If, on the other hand, you have the idea that it is the surroundings, or as we say today, the environment, which is determinant, you "dematerialize" or, in any case, "debiologize" the human race. At that moment you believe that by changing the environment you can change the inequalities among people and can even change and improve human beings. This picture becomes a social commitment and sends you off on marches and demonstrations.

There is not an ounce of science on either side. This is highly personal philosophy! The tragedy lies in the fact that governments can seize this philosophy and make it official. Think of the Nazis: we know to what systematic atrocities they were driven by their cult of the innate and the pseudobiology on which they sought to base it. But think too of the Soviets in the Stalin period: they stood out firmly for "nurture." They announced the coming of a "new man," the offspring of a classless society. But it must not be forgotten that in the USSR in the 1950s, posters appeared forbidding people to speak of "chromosomes" at a time when nowhere else in the world could their existence be doubted since they were being manipulated every day in the laboratory. Chromosomes were unable to obtain even a "visitor's visa" or, more precisely, were forbidden by dialectical materialism from existing, at the very time we were doing our first karyotype experiments in Marseille. In Bucharest I saw medical students who had to take a heavily weighted examination in Marxism. I happened to be visiting them at that time; I was stupefied initially, but then could not restrain a smile: some of them, before reciting their lessons in Marxism in front of the formidable panel of examiners, made the sign of the cross!

My dog was brought up in a home where people sang *Tosca* every day, but he never learned to sing *Tosca*! This is evidence that the genes have their say, if I may say so. But if you raise a cat as completely as possible in sensory isolation, its brain atrophies; and if on the contrary you place it in a setting where there is superstimulation by sound, affect, smell, taste, and vision, its brain will develop more than the average cat brain. This is the function of epigenesis. It is the environment which builds the apparatus for perceiving the world; but the foundation for this building is the chromosome, the initial promise of the cat brain. And the environment produces a thousand different cat brains every day, which will always be cat brains. Scientists say that the constitution of every animal's world is subject to two constraints: genetic and epigenetic.

To insert an "either-or" alternative—genesis or epigenesis—into this dual constraint in order to dissociate the terms, is to walk into a conceptual dead end. Perhaps the stubbornness with which we lose ourselves in these blind alleys can be ascribed to the two-way opposition we cultivate from childhood: anyone who is not tall is short; anyone who is not a man is a woman; and so forth. In the end, our most deeply held philosophies would succumb to this infantile dichotomy.

By contrast, ethology combines its conclusions with those of neurobiology to spotlight the extraordinary plasticity of the human brain and make the most of the fact that the dual constraint game is always an option. While nothing is erased, nothing is ever definitive in the development of the human person. Perhaps its most unequivocal clarifications thus far have been brought to the issue of perception: indeed we have discovered that any perception is not mere receptiveness but a selective activity, and that the structure of the perceiving apparatus is interdependent with the act of perceiving. However, to demonstrate this we have to use methods which themselves shape our perception, use instruments (films, tape recorders, frequency analyzers, and VCRs), and work out reproducible observation protocols that allow us to avoid the traps of naive observation and see our way clearly through the original jumble.

Let us visit our monkeys one last time. Every evening, you see a troop of macaques post a "lookout." We know that monkeys have a social organization which includes a group of dominant males. The lookout is recruited from this group or "panel" of dominant monkeys. You see him draw himself upright, his penis turns red, his coat stays white, and his scrotum turns blue: all the colors of the flag! He looks around him; the other monkeys slow down, start to prepare their nests, males, females, and young, then everyone goes to sleep. That night he will be the one on watch to spot any enemies.

This extraordinary daily ritual can of course be explained by chemistry. The exterior signs of the lookout are brought about by secretion of a very simple hormone with which we are quite familiar: melatonin, which is produced at the base of the brain and whose peripheral receptors in males are the scrotum and the penis.

But how are we to account for the individualization of the lookout? Why is there only one every evening, and, although he is not always the same, why does he always belong to the dominant group of males? To understand, you have to observe the everyday life of the monkeys; then you discover that the chosen individual is the one who had the best day: he ate well, was not attacked, and may have won a few hierarchical tussles.

Indeed, a stressed, fatigued monkey secretes less melatonin. The above explanation accounts for the behavior observed, which has a very precise biological basis. Mere observation will tell you that this lookout gives a particular cry when an eagle is hovering in the sky. Then you see the group of monkeys dive to the ground in a fraction of a second. If a leopard shows up, the lookout gives another cry, and the troop immediately rushes up the trees.

You have to use a tape recorder to understand this amazing behavior. When you analyze the cries, you find that these two types do not have the same shape. All the biophysical components of the cries contribute to organizing a signal that differs according to which mortal enemy of the monkey is involved: the one that swoops down from the sky or the one who rises from below. This can be checked by reconstituting these cries artificially and playing them back to the monkeys: the flight behavior is reproduced identically in the absence of any real danger.

So you have to know how to observe animals, be inventive, and come up with a few homemade "tricks" to study their behavior.

One of these tricks used by most ethologists is to give the animals names! These are not the pranks of overgrown schoolboys or ill-controlled sentimentality. In fact, as soon as you name animals, you observe them far better. Call one macaque Napoleon, another Nietzsche, and another Brigitte Bardot; if there is one who is bald and pensive, call him Giscard, and it will be easier for you to describe their doings and gestures, and the relationships among them. This is the last concession to the anthropomorphism of specialists who do their utmost to rid themselves of it! They cannot shed it altogether because they are people and they speak, but they at least know that this trap exists.

If this is not exactly an experiment, one can say that it is a "guided observation." Not only do we have to steer our vision by a pre-prepared series of questions, but we have to be able to interpret what this vision picks up. Hence the important role we assign to the camera. We saw this when we were talking about the deer, the baby's smile, and the pointing of the finger. With the naked eye, you only see what you think you see. As soon as the camera comes into the picture, you see things that were right there in front of you and that you failed to notice. The use of the video camera and slow motion represents considerable progress from this point of view; these are the particle accelerators of ethology. How many after-the-fact "discoveries" have been made when we ran the tape again and again!

The methods of ethology thus contribute to the progress of knowledge. But we have seen that, coordinated with the practices of clinical psychiatry, they also lead to progress in the treatment of some of the gravest diseases.

A social worker had asked me to examine a little girl, the daughter of an incestuous relationship. Such births are more frequent than is generally thought, but to collect this information one has to use nonstandard methods. Often the pregnancies are disturbed. The young mother, bewildered and prostrated, is unable to take care of the infant at birth and the child is sometimes dying of "anaclitism": retarded development accompanied by sadness, mutism, anorexia, insomnia, and weight loss. Let's be quite clear: the baby has a mother, food, a house; seen from the outside, it has "everything it needs for happiness." But it is lacking what is most essential: a warm affective interaction. In this particular case, the pediatrician called in had noted alarming dehydration and undernutrition; he had the child admitted to pediatric intensive care. The little girl was saved, then returned to the family. A few weeks later, the child was again close to death. The pediatricians said: "The parents don't know how to look after this child; it's unnatural..." In fact, what this little girl had lacked was a "figure of attachment." I knew that to give the child the desire to communicate, but also to eat and drink, there had to be an affectionate parental presence. And I drew these ideas from my painstaking comparative observations on animals and infants! Many cases of anorexia have this diagnosis and are thus rooted in these deeply buried affective strata of the individual's formation.

It is by escaping the immediate constraints of impressions and stimuli from the outside world that the living being enters the world of meaning. Or, better stated, this "escape" constitutes its world, a world endowed with meaning. This "escape" has degrees which essentially follow those of the animal scale as we imagine it to be today. They can be called "degrees of freedom": the margin widens, the scope of meaning broadens as we "ascend" the scale from fish to chimpanzees. When we get to humans, we reach the highest degree we know: the world of human beings, mediated by language, is throughout a world of meaning. Even the "biological" reality of this being develops and functions under the aegis of meaning, from the time of birth, which we can see as a birth into meaning, an access to a coded network of meanings that have already determined birth as a meaningful event.

The structures of perceptive activity clearly show this freedom relative to space: proximity continues to loosen its grip. Time undergoes the same process, but with human beings the jump may be a bigger one still. Monkeys are probably capable of anticipation. We have just seen that one of their behaviors, that of the lookout, emerges from the history of the day just past. But the length of this time is still curtailed. In the case of humans, this history springs wide open, back to an infinite past and forward to an ever-receding horizon. Speech has an incredible emotive function which allows us to weep over an event that happened twenty years ago, or look forward to a situation that will not take place until ten years hence. Meaning, by injecting the absent into the present, can plunge into a past in which no boundaries can be seen, just as no boundaries are discerned in the future.

TABOO: SUCCESSFUL INCESTS

For an ethologist, there can be no doubt of human "freedom": this is not the theological and legal chimera of "free will" which is the chief feature attributed by philosophers to the soul; rather it is a material freedom which is expressed in human language competence, and which has its biological basis in the infinite plasticity of the brain and its neuron networks. In other words: while human development is certainly not free from all determination, the determinisms that are manifested are sequential, temporary, and revisable—hence innumerable. Any human determinism is momentary.

This is why it seems impossible for me to speak of the "human animality," as too many biologists today are tempted to do, following many of yesterday's ethologists, in the name of a "materialism" that is real but reduced to the congruous and necessary share—proper but inadequate.

That this is a fantasy is indicated by much historical testimony. Think of the foundlings at the *Innocenti* Hospital in Florence. The medallion figures of Andrea della Robbia show that their limbs were bound with swaddling clothes that were pulled as tight as possible, as prevailing opinion had it that if these children (who were close to nature) were not held in a restrained posture, their animality would emerge. The evidence, it was said, was that they crawl on all fours! An incontestable "fact" was misinterpreted, as tiny children and abandoned older ones crawl on all fours. We know that it is the lack of affection and not an irresistible animal drive that prevents them from venturing into the upright position.

This fantasy is probably particularly powerful in the Christian world where animals are never seen as an external danger to human beings but as an intimate threat. The idea of animality is associated with that of the Fall, and numerous "pedagogical" practices have been guided by the desire to thrust down this lurking animality, always ready to rise up. The battle between the Freudian id and superego fits well into this culture. This obsession probably dictated many kinds of conduct that we now believe to be overly restrictive. Perhaps it also explains why child care is constant and attentive in our civilization, because ethnologists have shown us, moreover, what the cost of deritualization has been for societies.

Thus the human world appears to be cultural in nature since a person without culture is not a natural being—rather a nonviable amputee. The human world is one of spatial and temporal "depth," because of the existence of speech. This is why ethologists are today turning increasingly to ethnologists and particularly to linguists, while remaining attentive to the results obtained by neurobiologists.

We know that the concept of "culture" is simply loaded with ambiguities. It will be remembered that Claude Lévi-Strauss qualified the incest taboo as "the basic step by which the transition from nature to culture is accomplished." This is hardly supported by our observations: We see scarcely any incest in animals but observe that it is extremely widespread in human beings—not only the "unhappy" incests that damage the lives of so many of our patients, male and female alike, but also the "successful" and "happy" incests that we hear little about.

A curious adventure is taking place with our description of loving incest. Norbert Sillamy was the first to propose the term "happy incest," but the evolution of the "couples" compelled us to make the term more precise and speak of "loving incest" rather than "happy incest"; we are well aware how love stories usually end, and incestuous love affairs cannot end in marriage. So they have to remain secret, outside the bounds of society, totally beautiful and intense . . . as long as the love lasts.

The hypothesis came to us during some observations of animal ethology from which we learned that a pair of animals without attachments could couple even if they were mother and son, while attached animals inhibited their sexual behavior even if they were not genetically related. Simple attachment inhibited sex.

We have found that this process of numbing of sexual desire has been manifested in many human couples since sex life expectancy has been increased by improvements in our technology.

Men continued to have nocturnal erections, proving their biological ability to have sexual intercourse, while they failed regularly in their attempts with the women they loved tenderly. Extramarital affairs went very well...at the risk of love and its destructive-reconstructive power. Falling in love at age twenty gives you the strength to leave your original family and embark on the building of a family by marriage. Falling in love at age fifty gives you the strength to leave your family by marriage and embark on creating another family by marriage. Yet, the ambience is not the same because the destruction-reconstruction does not take place at the same stage in life and does not have the same affective consequences.

Yet, animal experimentation raises an important theoretical issue, confirmed by human clinical observation: attachment numbs desire.

Hence the hypothesis that emerges from this theoretical question: when relatives are unable to weave an attachment, nothing stands in the way of their gratifying their sexual desires, not even the incest taboo.

I was amazed by the speed with which we gathered the clinical information that confirmed this hypothesis. Brothers and sisters separated for a long period of time, when they found themselves once again under the same roof, saw each other as two desirable young people. They were neither numbed by an attachment nor halted by taboo. But this loving incest is not happy. Most such couples separate after a love affair. They often part after a deliberate falling-out, frequently without explanation, and never speak of it again, even between themselves.

Yet, certain couples conceal this secret love in the depths of their beings. They live in secrecy under assumed names. Sometimes they marry another to force a separation, but keep an intense affection for the incestuous other.

Incests between father-in-law and daughter support this hypothesis, so frequent are they. But even our own Western culture has not always labeled these sexual encounters as incestuous, and Molière (1622–1673) tells us that a stepfather can marry his stepdaughter perfectly legally when his wife dies, something that was not infrequent at the time. This shows how "incest" is a word that refers to types of relationship that differ to astonishing degrees from culture to culture.

Father-daughter incest is more frequent than is generally believed. I am not speaking of the sadistic, drunken, brutal incests that turn into scandals when they become known. I am speaking of loving incests where we always see that there has been a disruption in the attachment because the separation was total or because separations were repeated at close intervals or because, in families with incestuous relations, the attachment was poorly woven, thus authorizing sexual acts.

What surprised us most were the accounts we collected of mother-son incestuous acts, repeated over a number of years in the course of a veritable love affair.

Here again, these incests ended in separations when the sons fell in love with someone else. Yet the emotional color of the parting differed greatly according to sex. When daughters fell in love with someone else, they began to loathe their fathers as if a second love affair were needed to confer the meaning of incest on the first. These women often explain that the intensity of the affair was so great that they had not realized it was incestuous!

Incestuous sons have milder and quieter reactions. When they fall in love with someone else, they leave their mother-lovers in secret, without reproach, with a kind of nostalgia and even gratitude in the depths of their hearts that will remain a secret forever.

How far we are from theory! No violence here, or rarely. No psychosis either, as Freud had hoped for.

There are two unanswered questions in this work which is still ongoing: when I speak in public of my hypothesis that grew from ethologic studies, I am immediately contacted in my office by persons or couples who come to confirm the validity of this hypothesis and the never-written and never-thought-of consequences of this loving incest.

But what was most striking to me was the reaction of professional psychologists when I apprised them of this information: they denied it!

One young woman who attended one of my lectures on this subject could not restrain herself from turning to her boyfriend, a doctor, and saying: "This was something that happened to me." Her friend replied: "That's impossible—you must have dreamt it."

When a fact escapes the culture, social thinking must reject it to retain consistency. Rather than change the theory by assimilating the new fact, social thinking dismisses the fact to save the theory.

The incest taboo is very important for us as a reflection of the foundations of our societies, and so the taboo against incest is also a taboo against speaking about it.

This way of thinking, or rather theorizing, of tidying up facts to provide us with a consistent and stable view of the world and prevent any changes that would be too distressing or too tiring, explains the possibility of totalitarian theories which, at least, provide unchanging truths and absolute certainties.

When Bruno Bettelheim entered the concentration camps after World War II and wished to report on what he had seen, most American magazine editors rejected his articles, with the explanation that his pain must have made him exaggerate the facts.

THE HUMAN ADVENTURE OF SPEECH

It seems to me that the work of many ethnologists over these past few years has raised questions about the soundness and universality of Lévi-Strauss's criterion. Let us content ourselves with accepting an idea of culture that links it directly to the birth of speech and the socially coded behavioral clusters that support it. Sociologists and linguists have provided confirmation for many clinical observations: it seems that the act of speech is indissociable from specific gestures, feelings, and behaviors. Take conversational rituals, just as an example: the direction of the gaze, nods, silences, interruptions, and synchronizations, and the positions and movements of the hands. Each of the elements involved in the scenario is socially coded. Thus one can draw "speaker profiles" using the position of the head, the general posture of the body, and the placement of the hands as pertinent features. Certain gestures have an almost universal signing value, such as obscene gestures. But there is also a large number of "cultural requirements." We know, for example, that for the Japanese, looking someone straight in the eye is a sign not of openness but of the greatest vulgarity. From one end of the Earth to the other, meanings shift and sometimes even reverse. This is why diplomacy has always been a very subtle art of interpretation. Individual variations are established within one culture, signifying the existence of types of personality. In Western countries, for example, we have men who interrupt and "cut each other off"; when two interrupters meet, a rivalry ensues. The cut-off interrupter tries to recoup by incorporating what his interrupter has just said into his own speech. Women, on the other hand, do not interrupt. They do not compete; they wait, then speak of something else.

Such observations are confirmed in clinical practice: when you speak to a psychotic patient, the conversational gestures are not the same. The patient's eyes are cast fixedly downward, there are dead silences, and subjects of conversation are interrupted. The interviews are exhausting for the psychotherapist. The psychotic patient will tell you that the therapist is crazy, because he or she sidesteps the questions the patient asks. Obsessives speak very slowly and fluently, without a pause, but their speech is monotonous and they stare at you the entire time. They never give you a break by shifting their eyes from you. You begin to feel that they're "beating about the bush" and will never get to the point. And when you try to speak to bring the conversation back to the subject, they'll raise their voices to stop you. Hysterics, on the other hand, seem more intense in their conversations because of their exuberant gestures and very strong synchronizations which attempt to trigger strong emotional contagiousness by underlining words with gestures. When the conversation is over, you find that there was more emotion than information in what transpired. The structure of the conversation and the way in which people talk thus play a part in the emotional contagiousness of speech.

Here we are not dealing with the disembodied speech which so easily creates a sense of the sacred because of its fantastic and fleeting ability to evoke things that are totally absent. This type of speech is the speech of those committed to the religious life.

Ethologic speech, on the other hand, is embodied. It is composed of sounds and melodies punctuated by silences, with an accompanying text of facial expressions that convey verbal emotions, gestures that underline or "contradict" the words, and postures that shape space into speech.

Psychoanalytic speech is perhaps somewhere in between the two, with the sacred effect it induces by evoking an absent world and the affective effect it brings about by causing past emotions to be relived and by transferring them, then and there, to an absent presence.

By converting an ethologic object into speech, the observer tries to render observable how two talking beings go about talking to each other, and the form that the communication takes.

But the fact of introducing history into our observations and the comparison between living species brings us to frame the question about speech in different terms: newborn human beings are speechless to begin with, fascinated as they might be by the speech of those who care for them, and most living beings have developed communicative tools other than words. This brings us to the following question in ethology: how do you go about communicating when you are not human and how do you go about communicating when you are a speechless human?

Animal semiotics has given us a way of analyzing a corpus of animal communications that describes a behavioral syntax composed of visual signals such as the color of the blue and red feathers of kingfishers, the yellow and red color combination on the beaks of gulls, the lucifer-like phosphorescence of the bellies of female earthworms, and the heart-shaped white spot on the rump of a gazelle. The voluminous postures of dominant males, the submissive gestures of consenting females, and the threatening expressions of mammals that bare their teeth, are a veritable repertoire of signals whose varied combinations can compose highly rich and complex messages.

Olfactory signals allow remote "touching" when a molecule penetrates and touches the nose of a mammal; contact allows close touching when a large monkey touches the hand of another intimidated monkey, or touches the genitals of a female to reassure her, or takes a baby monkey by the chin to get its attention.

Acoustic signals fill the atmosphere where each species gives sound extremely variable forms, where the intensity, rhythm, repetition, change, frequency, and amplitude create veritable symphonies whose function it is to transmit information and emotions over a distance.

These signals are connected together, organized, and harmonized to enable both participants in the communication to synchronize themselves as pragmatic evidence of animal semiology.

Hence animals can communicate with great richness, highly organized in different internal worlds, which are sometimes even individual: the ballad of a finch may end in a trill that characterizes that particular singer, an actual sung signature of the individual.

Yet, while linguists permit us to say that the syntax and pragmatics of communication truly offer an enormous richness and expressive poetry to animals, they advise us to be more reserved about animal semantics: the scope of what can be signified or referred to is modest in nonhuman worlds. No nonhuman living being is able to transmit information with reference to a totally absent event. Whatever stimulates communication must be close in time and space. No finch can sing the song of the French finch that drove the English finch out of Normandy at the end of the 15th century. Finches have no history and their songs are extraordinarily rich in varied information. No ape can make the gestures that criticize the thoughts of another ape, even though these two apes may be more fluent in Ameslan than I.

The language and thoughts of animals are rooted in context.

How is it that a human being is capable of shaping the noises emitted by the human mouth into meanings so as to create, by this unlikely trick, a totally absent world that is utterly nonexistent in the context?

My dog turns emotions into meaning, and when he growls all human beings understand the canine message, whatever their native tongue. My dog communicates his intentions rather well, and everyone understands him when he wants to go out, eat, play, be petted, or even be forgiven. However, he has never expressed his shame at being a mongrel; one day when he was feeling "in the pink," quite secure in his territory, and reinforced by the love of his masters, I saw him face down a purebred and extremely expensive dog.

And yet a speechless person does not live in a dog's world, but continues to live in a world of human beings. Such a person is unable to speak, but can still communicate, since the ethologic approach to speech allows us to argue that thoughts can exist without words. They are organized around images, and an understanding takes place in a sequence of images where, however, objects remain human objects.

The increased life expectancy we are currently seeing in Western nations is allowing us to perform a very frequent and natural experiment when the left sylvian artery becomes temporarily blocked. Since it supplies blood to the speech area of the brain, the patient loses the ability to speak for a few hours and then, when the artery is unclogged, is able to speak once again.

When asked what went on in the mind during these few speechless hours, the patient is highly astonished, and routinely replies that it was like being in a silent movie: one understood what was going on, but could reply only by gestural signs. The patient attempts to convey some meaning in signs but was often unable to do so. The ethologist then observes, as the patient becomes frustrated, that the face and body are still able to express the emotions in the emotional repertoire of the human species: when the use of conventional signs has been lost, the body is still able to express the universal signs of all human beings.

This very simple observation in neurology somewhat modifies our veneration for speech. What distinguishes humans from nonhumans is not so much speech considered in its material form as an acoustic object which then belongs to any living being; it is mainly the human being's incredible aptitude for imparting meaning.

For most of us, then, anything can make a sign: a thing can be transformed into a historized object, a noise can be organized into music or a word, a color can be arranged to make a picture, a series of ges-

111

tures can be incorporated into a dance or a theatrical performance. This power which opens the gate to a totally absent world can impregnate a number of informational items that are ridiculously present. Matter, shrunk to its proper size, enters into resonance with signs to create the immaterial. But this matter is essential: first of all, before I can speak, the development of my human brain must be properly programmed; my eyes must encounter a figure of attachment to make me want to speak, and I must soak up the speech bath of the adults around me.

This new ethological look at speech changes its status: speech no longer falls from the heavens: it becomes rooted in the body, affectivity, and social life.

What conclusions may we draw from these observations, if not that human beings considered as individuals are social beings; and that our individuality is formed only in a field of affective tensions structured by words? Any philosophy or psychology that is unaware of this will go astray. If human nature consists in being "cultural" in the sense in which we have stated it, we can understand that being alone is simply not living. We can also make a judgment on such moral attitudes of "self-centeredness" which are common currency these days. Thus, human ethology carries its own "ethic," but this remains a subject for future discussion.

BIBLIOGRAPHY

CHALLAMEL, M. J. and LAHLOU, S., "Sleep and Smiling in the Neonate: a New Approach," *Sleep Research Society* **7** (IX), 1984.

COSNIER, J. and BROSSARD, A., *La Communication non verbale* [Non-verbal communication], Neûchatel/Paris, Delachaux & Niestlé, 1984.

COSNIER, J. and KERBRAT-ORECCHIONI, C., *Décrire la conversation* [Describe the conversation], Presses universitaires de Lyon, Lyon, 1987.

COULON, J., "La communication animale" [Animal communication] in COSNIER, J., COULON, J., BERREDENDONNER, A., ORECCHIONI, C., *Les Voies du langage* [The paths of language], Dunod, Paris, 1982.

CYRULNIK, B., *Sous le signe du lien* [Under the sign of the link], Hachette, Paris, 1989.

CYRULNIK, B., FORZY, M., and VERRIER, J. P., "Face à face, biches et enfants psychotiques" [Female deer and psychotic children face to face],

International congress *L'Homme et l'animal*, Monaco, 1990.

CYRULNIK, B. and LEROY, R., "Éthologie des objets d'attachement" [The ethology of objects of attachment], *Psycho. méd.* **2**:275–278, 1988.

DASSER, V., "Animal behaviour," in *Vauclair*, pp. 225–230, 1988.

DELACOUR, J., *Apprentissage et Mémoire, une approche neurobiologique* [Learning and memory, a neurobiological approach], Masson, Paris, 1987.

DEPUTTE, B., "L'évitement de l'inceste chez les primates" [Avoidance of incest among primates], *La Recherche*, Nov. 1987.

DORE, F. Y., *L'Apprentissage, une approche psycho-éthologique* [Learning, a psychoethological approach], Maloine, Montréal, 1988.

EIBL-EIBESFELDT, I., *Éthologie-Biologie du comportement* [The ethobiology of behavior], Éditions Scientifiques, Paris, 1987.

HENRIOT, P., "Une étude en milieu psychiatrique d'éthologie clinique de l'olfaction dans ses rapports aux souvenirs," [A study of clinical ethology of olfaction in its relationship to memories in a psychiatric environment], a CES thesis in psychiatry, Marseille, 1991.

MALSON, L., *Les Enfants sauvages* [Wild children], Union générale d'éditions (coll. 10/18), Paris, 1964.

MONTAGNER, H., *L'Attachement. Les débuts de la tendresse* [Attachment. The beginnings of tenderness], Éd. Odile Jacob, Paris, 1988.

ROBICHEZ-DISPA, A., "Observation d'une relation médiatisée par l'objet chez l'enfant pré-verbalisant" [A case of object-indicated relationship in a preverbal child], University thesis, Aix-Marseille-II, June, 1988.

SCHAAL, B., "Olfaction in Infants and Children: Developmental and Functional Perspectives," *Chemical Senses* 2(13):145–190, 1988.

TINBERGEN, N., *L'Univers du goéland argenté* [The universe of the herring gull], Elsevier, Paris, 1975.